CONTENTS

Chapter 4 CHILD MAINTENANCE AND SCHEDULE 1 CHILDREN ACT 1989

Chapter 5 DOMESTIC VIOLENCE AND HARASSMENT

Chapter 6 INTRODUCTION TO THE CHILDREN ACT 1989

Chapter 7 PARENTAL RESPONSIBILITY

Chapter 8 PRIVATE CHILD LAW

Chapter 9 CHILDREN IN NEED

Chapter 10 EMERGENCY CHILD PROTECTION

Chapter 11 CARE AND SUPERVISION ORDERS

Chapter 12 CHALLENGING A LOCAL AUTHORITY'S ACTIONS

Chapter 13 ADOPTION AND SPECIAL GUARDIANSHIP

TABLE OF CASES

PREFACE

The Key Cases series is designed to give a clear understanding of important cases. This is useful when studying a new topic and invaluable as a revision aid.

Each case is broken down into fact and law. In addition many cases are extended by the use of important extracts from the judgment or by comment or by highlighting problems. In some instances students are reminded that there is a link to other cases or material. If the link case is in another part of the same Key Cases book, the reference will be clearly shown. Some links will be to additional cases or materials that do not feature in the book.

To give a clear layout, symbols have been used at the start of each component of the case. The symbols are:

 Key Facts – These are the basic facts of the case.

 Key Law – This is the major principle of law in the case, the *ratio decidendi*.

 Key Judgment – This is an actual extract from a judgment made on the case.

 Key Comment – Influential or appropriate comments made on the case.

 Key Problem – Apparent inconsistencies or difficulties in the law.

 Key Link – This indicates other cases in the text which should be considered with this case.

The Key Link symbol alerts readers to links within the book and also to cases and other material especially statutory provisions which is not included.

At the start of each chapter there are mind maps highlighting the main cases and points of law. In addition, within most chapters, one or two of the most important cases are boxed to identify them and stress their importance.

Each Key Cases book can be used in conjunction with the Key Facts book on the same subject. Equally they can be used as additional material to support any other textbook.

The law is stated as I believe it to be on 1st August 2007.

Helen L. Conway

VALIDITY OF MARRIAGE AND CIVIL PARTNERSHIPS

GENDER AND ABILITY TO FORM A RECOGNISED UNION

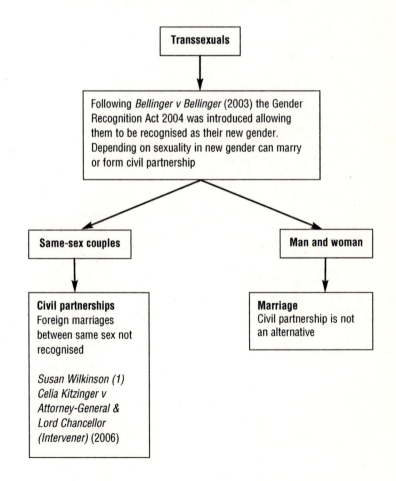

Transsexuals

Following *Bellinger v Bellinger* (2003) the Gender Recognition Act 2004 was introduced allowing them to be recognised as their new gender. Depending on sexuality in new gender can marry or form civil partnership

Same-sex couples

Man and woman

Civil partnerships
Foreign marriages between same sex not recognised

Susan Wilkinson (1) Celia Kitzinger v Attorney-General & Lord Chancellor (Intervener) (2006)

Marriage
Civil partnership is not an alternative

1.1 Transsexuals and marriage

HC *Corbett v Corbett (otherwise Ashley)* [1970] 2 All ER 33

At the time of marriage the petitioner knew that the respondent had been registered at birth as a male and had undergone a sex-change operation which included the construction of an artificial vagina. He sought a decree of nullity on the grounds that the 'wife' was male. The respondent said that the petition should be founded on the husband's wilful refusal to consummate.

The respondent was of the male chromosomal sex, of male gonadal sex, of male genital sex and psychologically a transsexual. She was not female and the marriage was void. Even if it had been valid she was physically incapable of consummation, as using the completely artificial cavity could never constitute true intercourse.

A person's biological sex was fixed at birth.

W v W (Nullity: Gender) [2001] 1 FLR 324 HC, see **1.4**.

Goodwin & I v UK [2002] 2 FLR 487 ECHR.

HL *Bellinger v Bellinger* [2003] UKHL 21; [2003] 1 FLR 1043

The government's failure to alter the birth certificates of transsexual people or to allow them to marry in their new gender role was a breach of the European Convention on Human Rights.

A male-to-female transsexual married a man and sought a declaration that the marriage was valid and a declaration that that s 11(c) of the Matrimonial Causes Act 1973 was incompatible with Arts 8 and 12 of the European Convention on the Protection of Human Rights and Fundamental Freedoms 1950.

Corbett v Corbett had not been followed in other EU countries, but the issue of gender reassignment was a matter for Parliament, not the courts, to deal with. A declaration was granted. Section 11(c) was clearly incompatible with Arts 8 and 12.

These cases led to the introduction of the Gender Recognition Act 2004.

1.2 Civil partnerships

HL *Susan Wilkinson (1) Celia Kitzinger v Attorney-General & Lord Chancellor (Intervener)* [2006] EWHC 2022 (Fam)

Two woman were married in Canada. They applied for UK recognition of their marriage under s 55 Family Law Act 1986, not being satisfied with a civil partnership.

The declaration was refused.

Sir Mark Potter

'The intention of the government in introducing the [civil partnership] legislation was not to create a "second class" institution, but a parallel and equalising institution designed to redress a perceived inequality of treatment of long-term monogamous same-sex relationships, while at the same time, demonstrating support for the long-established institution of marriage.'

1.3 Nullity: wilful refusal to consummate

HC *J v J* [1946] 2 All ER 760

The husband had an operation which rendered him able to have intercourse but not to impregnate his wife.

The husband was not consummating the marriage by his acts of intercourse, as he had prevented the intercourse from having its natural consequence 'in the passage of male seed into the body of the woman'. As he had brought about a 'structural defect in his organs of generation' by his own decision, this amounted to wilful refusal to consummate.

HL *Horton v Horton* [1946] 2 All ER 871

The husband was in the army, so opportunity for sexual intercourse was limited to his leave periods. The parties were

Roman Catholic and the husband suggested that they should leave children until they had their own house, and as contraception was not an option, that they refrain. Although the wife agreed with some disappointment, later attempts at intercourse by the husband were rebuffed.

The words 'wilful refusal to consummate' connote a settled and definite decision arrived at without just excuse, and in determining that the court should have regard to the whole history of the marriage. In the circumstances, the wife had not refused wilfully.

CA *Kaur v Singh* [1972] 1 All ER 292

A Sikh couple married at a registry office. The husband then refused to go through the religious marriage ceremony which was necessary to fully marry under the Sikh religion.

The wife was granted a decree of nullity: the husband had failed to implement the marriage and in doing so had wilfully failed to consummate it.

HC *A v J (Nullity Proceedings)* [1989] 1 FLR 110

An Indian couple entered into an arranged marriage. A quick civil ceremony was arranged for immigration purposes, with a religious ceremony to follow some months later, after which they would cohabit. The wife was unimpressed with the husband in the days after the civil ceremony and refused to enter into the second ceremony. He explained that he had assumed her family would want him to be very formal to her until the religious ceremony.

Because the religious ceremony was for this couple an essential condition of cohabitation, it was right to treat the wife's refusal to accept the husband's apologies and to enter into the religious ceremony as wilful refusal.

1.4 Nullity: not male and female

HC *W v W (Nullity: Gender)* [2001] I FLR 324

The husband sought a decree of nullity on the basis that the wife was not at the time of marriage a woman. The wife had been born with indeterminate sex and had been registered as a boy. However at 15 she developed a female body shape and as an adult lived as a woman. Surgery was needed to allow her to have sexual intercourse. The woman's chromosomal and gonadal sex was male, the appearance of her external genitalia was ambiguous, so that she was neither a normal man nor woman, and her general appearance from early teens, plus her gender orientation, was female.

This was a case of physical intersex, not trans-sexuality like *Corbett v Corbett.* The chromosomal, gonadal and genital characteristics were not congruent and the *Corbett* test was not passed. She was female for the purposes of her marriage.

1.5 Nullity: duress

HC *Silver (otherwise Kraft) v Silver* [1955] 2 All ER 614

A German woman wished to live with an English man (AS), who was already married. In order to get her into England she entered into a marriage with AS's step-brother, who then formed another relationship. Many years later when she wished to remarry she sought a decree of nullity on the grounds of lack of consent.

The mere fact that she needed the marriage for immigration purposes did not amount to duress, so the nullity decree was rejected. Nevertheless, a divorce was granted.

CA *Hirani v Hirani* (1983) 4 FLR 232

A Hindu girl formed a relationship with a Muslim. Her parents found this abhorrent, and arranged a marriage to a Hindu whom the family had never met. It was not consummated. The wife sought nullity on the grounds of duress, because her parents had threatened to turn her out of the home if she did not go through with it. At first instance it was held that there was no threat to life and limb, and so no duress.

Duress is a coercion of the will so as to vitiate consent. The question is whether the threats or pressure were such as to overbear the will of the individual and destroy the reality of consent. Here, the parental threats had vitiated consent.

CA *Singh v Singh* [1971] 2 All ER 828

A Sikh girl entered into an arranged marriage. Against her wishes she went to the register office ceremony but then refused the religious ceremony.

In order to establish that there had been duress which vitiated consent to the marriage, a petitioner would have to show that their will was overborne by genuine fear induced by threats of immediate danger to life, limb or liberty. The girl had acted out of respect for her parents and her religion, there were no such threats and hence no duress.

HC *P v R (Forced Marriage: Annulment: Procedure)* [2003] 1 FLR 631

A woman was forced into a marriage whilst visiting Pakistan for a funeral.

The woman's consent was vitiated by the force exerted by her parents, both physical and emotional.

1.6 Nullity: mental disorder

HC *Bennett v Bennett* [1969] 1 All ER 539

Unknown to the husband, the wife had twice been admitted for short periods to a mental hospital before the marriage. She was admitted again for a very short time during the marriage. The husband, who had been apart from the wife for most of the time, being on active service overseas, sought a decree of nullity.

The temporary incidents of insanity and unsoundness of mind did not constitute evidence that she was suffering from a mental disorder of such a kind to make her unfit for marriage and the procreation of children.

CHAPTER 2

DIVORCE

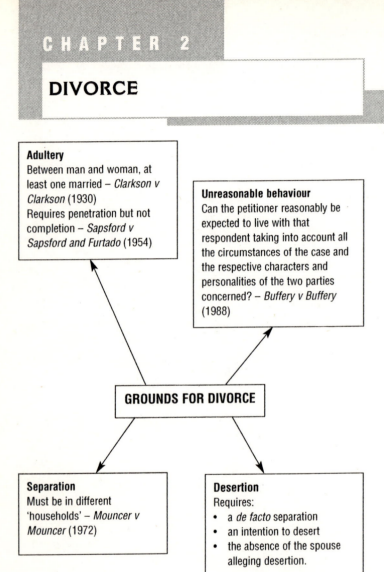

Adultery
Between man and woman, at least one married – *Clarkson v Clarkson* (1930)
Requires penetration but not completion – *Sapsford v Sapsford and Furtado* (1954)

Unreasonable behaviour
Can the petitioner reasonably be expected to live with that respondent taking into account all the circumstances of the case and the respective characters and personalities of the two parties concerned? – *Buffery v Buffery* (1988)

GROUNDS FOR DIVORCE

Separation
Must be in different 'households' – *Mouncer v Mouncer* (1972)

Desertion
Requires:
- a *de facto* separation
- an intention to desert
- the absence of the spouse alleging desertion.

Pardy v Pardy (1939)

2.1 Adultery

HC *Clarkson v Clarkson* (1930) 143 LT 775, 46 TLR 623

Adultery is the voluntary sexual intercourse between a man and a woman who are not married to each other but one of whom at least is a married person.

HC *Sapsford v Sapsford and Furtado* [1954] 2 All ER 373

Adultery requires an act of penetration but does not require the completion of sexual intercourse.

Cleary v Cleary [1974] 1 WLR 73

It is necessary for the petitioner to find it intolerable to live with the respondent who has committed adultery. However, the intolerability need not be linked to the adultery.

2.2 Unreasonable behaviour

CA *Buffery v Buffery* [1988] 2 FLR 365

A divorce under s 1(2)(b) MCA 1973 was refused because the respondent husband had not been guilty of conduct of a 'grave and weighty' nature and the parties had simply drifted apart.

The correct test was that in the earlier case of whether a right-thinking person, looking at the particular husband and wife, would ask whether the petitioner could reasonably be expected to live with that respondent, taking into account all the circumstances of the case and the respective characters and personalities of the two parties concerned. The conduct did not have to be 'grave and weighty'.

→

Livingstone Stallard v Livingston Stallard [1974] Fam 47, CA – the case in which this test was first formulated.

2.3 Separation

HC **Mouncer v Mouncer** [1972] 1 All ER 334

The unhappy spouses had separate bedrooms. They ate together and both cleaned the whole house, but the wife did not wash the husband's clothes. The husband stayed to be with the children. After they had grown up he sought a divorce on the grounds that he and his wife had been living apart for two years.

If a couple – as here – were sharing the same household, the rejection of a normal physical relationship coupled with an absence of normal affection was not sufficient to constitute living apart.

2.4 Desertion

CA *Pardy v Pardy* [1939] 3 All ER 779

The requirements for desertion are a *de facto* separation, an intention by the respondent to desert and the absence of consent of the spouse of the person alleging desertion. Desertion can begin after a period of mutual separation from the time when those requirements begin to exist.

2.5 Grave financial or other hardship

CA *Le Marchant v Le Marchant* [1977] 3 All ER 610

A wife claimed a divorce would cause her grave financial hardship, because she would lose her husband's post office widow's pension.

Where the answer to a petition set up a *prima facie* case of grave financial hardship under s 5 of the 1973 Act, the proper approach was that the petition should be dismissed, unless in his reply the petitioner met the answer by putting forward reasonable proposals, acceptable to the court, which were sufficient to remove the financial hardship pleaded.

The facts of this case would now be resolved by legislation allowing pension attachment or earmarking.

CHAPTER 3

FINANCES AFTER DIVORCE/DISSOLUTION OF CIVIL PARTNERSHIP

THE HISTORICAL APPROACH TO DIVISION OF ASSETS

The One Third Rule
Wachtel v Wachtel (1973)

Divide by three and give wife and children one-third

↓

Reasonable requirements
Preston v Preston (1981)
Dart v Dart (1996)

Award based on needs founded upon homes, children and lifestyle.

↓

Yardstick of equality
White v White (2000)

Calculate a settlement based on all the s 25 criteria then check if the percentage result deviates from 50%. Such deviation is permitted only if there is a reason that does not discrimate between home maker and breadwinner.

↓

Four principles of fairness
Miller v Miller (2006)
McFarlane v McFarlane (2006)

1. Welfare of the children
2. Needs of adults
3. Compensation
4. Sharing

3.1 Interests of the children

HC *Chaimberlain v Chaimberlain* [1973] 1 WLR 1557

The court must only put the interest of the children first for so long as they are minors.

3.2 The old one-third rule

CA *Wachtel v Wachtel* [1973] 1 All ER 829

The court, dealing with a divorcing couple, set out various principles to interpret the then Matrimonial Proceedings and Property Act 1970.

The fairest starting point is to give the wife and children one-third of the capital assets and one-third of the parties' joint earnings. That was not a rule, and might not be applicable where the wife could work because there were no children, or if the marriage had only lasted a short time.

Although this rule has long been disproved, in *Miller v Miller* [2006] UKHL 24, by coincidence, the wife still got one-third of the capital. The wife in *McFarlane v McFarlane* [2006] UKHL 24 received a third of her husband's income.

Dart v Dart [1996] 2 FLR 286 CA, see **3.3**.

3.3 The old 'needs' basis

 Preston v Preston (1981) 2 FLR 331

The court disagreed that a millionaire husband should give his wife only the matrimonial home and £250,000, because whilst it amply met her needs, that was not the only consideration under s 25 MCA 1973. A lump sum of £600,000 was ordered. The husband appealed.

Where the available resources were very large, there would be a maximum sum which would satisfy all the wife's legitimate claims, and there would be a point beyond which the wealth of the husband became irrelevant.

CA *Dart v Dart* [1996] 2 FLR 286

The parties were extremely wealthy. The husband agreed he could pay whatever order was made against him. The wife claimed a house in the US and £122 million. She received the house and £9 million, and appealed.

The court, when considering financial provision for a wife who had made no direct contribution to the husband's wealth, had to declare the boundary between the wife's reasonable and unreasonable requirements. There was no justification for applying a mathematical solution – one-third or one-half, as suggested in *Wachtel v Wachtel* – and to do so would be inconsistent with the guidance consistently given by the Court of Appeal in cases dating back to 1976. The correct test was to calculate what a spouse reasonably required, whilst having regard to the other criteria mentioned in s 25(2) Matrimonial Causes Act 1973. There is no justification for making an award going beyond the spouse's need founded upon homes, children and lifestyle. Redistribution of capital outside that requirement is not within the statutory provisions.

Butler-Sloss LJ

'I am sure that any change in the way in which the courts should decide money cases ought to be by legislation . . . I wonder whether the courts may not have imposed too restrictive an interpretation upon the words of s 25 and given too great weight to reasonable requirements over other criteria set out in the section . . . '

HC *Conran v Conran* **[1997] 2 FLR 615**

At the time of divorce the assets of the wife were £4.3 million. The husband had £80 million. She sought a lump sum of £8.9 million. The wife had played an active role in the home, as hostess, and by her journalism promoting the husband's business interests. The case turned on whether these contributions should be looked at when determining the wife's reasonable requirements.

Contributions were outside the compass of the phrase 'reasonable requirements', as it was difficult to fit an allowance for contribution into an analysis of a wife's needs. The court should survey the wife's reasonable requirements and then place her contribution and all other factors into the balance, taking into account the nexus between the contribution and the creation of the resources. She was awarded a lump sum of £6.2 million.

3.4 The current approach

HL *White v White* [2000] 2 FLR 981

Mr and Mrs White had been married for 36 years. They farmed. They had assets of £4.3 million, £193,000 of which was in the wife's sole name while £1,783,500 was in the husband's sole name. The balance was in their joint names. The joint assets included a farm in respect of which there was a joint partnership deed. The wife applied for ancillary relief. The High Court awarded her needs only in the sum of £980,000. On appeal the Court of Appeal again restricted her to her needs, at a higher figure of £1.5 million. The effect was that the husband got his needs and all the surplus. The wife appealed to the House of Lords.

(1) There is no presumption of equal division of assets as a starting point.

(2) However, the parties should be treated with equality. No distinction should be made in terms of the value of contributions between a home-making role and a bread-winning role.

(3) The approach should be to weigh in the balance all the s 25 criteria, then use 'the cross-check of equality' to ensure that neither spouse was discriminated against by reason of

their gender or the role they took in the marriage.

(4) It is incorrect to limit a spouse to their 'reasonable requirements'.

Lord Nicholls

'As a general guide, equality should be departed from only if, and to the extent that, there is good reason for doing so. The need to consider and articulate reasons for departing from equality would help the parties and the court to focus on the need to ensure the absence of discrimination. . .

On the facts of the case there may be a good reason why the wife should be confined to her needs and the husband left with the much larger balance. But the mere absence of financial need cannot by itself be a sufficient reason. If it were, discrimination would be creeping in by the back door, In these cases, it should be remembered, the claimant is usually the wife. Hence the importance of the cross-check against the yardstick of equal division.'

HL | *McFarlane v McFarlane* [2006] UKHL 24, [2006] 1 FLR 1186

Miller v Miller [2006] UKHL 24, see **3.3**.

The court must do what is fair. Fairness has four elements:

(1) The needs of the children must be met.

(2) The needs of the parties must be met. In many cases the resources run out at that point, and the search for fairness ends.

(3) There may be an element of compensation where disparity of earning capacity results from the way the parties conducted their marriage.

(4) Sharing. Each is entitled to an equal share of the assets unless there is good reason to the contrary.

There is no invariable rule as to whether once needs are met you share then compensate, or vice versa.

Lord Nicholls

'Fairness is an elusive concept. It is an instinctive response to a given set of facts. Ultimately it is grounded in social and moral values. These values or attitudes can be stated. But they cannot be justified or refuted by any objective process of logical reasoning. Moreover they change from one generation to the next. It is not surprising therefore that in the present context there can be different views on the requirements of fairness in any particular case.'

3.5 Special contributions

CA *Cowan v Cowan* [2001] 2 FLR 19

The couple had £11.5 million. After a 35-year marriage the wife sought an equal share, claiming that indirectly via her role as wife and mother she had contributed to the success of the companies. The husband said the outcome was fairness, not equality, and his 'stellar contributions' should be recognised, as should the fact that he needed capital to run the business and that he held some assets on trust for his brother. He also argued that much of the wealth came after separation, and was not available for division.

The wife was not limited to her reasonable requirements, but *White v White* did not require equal division. The factors raised by the husband including recognition of his 'business genius' justified a departure from equality. The wife got 38 per cent of the assets. The assets are to be valued at the time of trial except exceptionally where one party had wasted or dissipated assets prior to trial.

HL *H v H (Financial Provisions: Special Contribution)* [2002] 2 FLR 1021

The husband was a highly successful partner in a firm of solicitors, and had made money collecting works of art. He argued a special contribution which he failed to establish.

In assessing whether there was a special contribution, the relevant question was 'What did the parties expect when they set out on their lives together. Have their lives taken a course neither of them would have expected and led to riches neither of them would have contemplated?'

CA *Lambert v Lambert* [2003] 1 FLR 139

The husband sold his business during the marriage, for £26 million. The wife sought an equal share of assets at divorce.

The husband argued for more because he had shown exceptional business flair and negotiating skills. At first instance the wife got 37 per cent and appealed.

(1) Special contribution remained a legitimate possibility, but only in exceptional circumstances, and not in this case. A good idea, initiative, entrepreneurial skill and extensive hard work were insufficient to establish special contribution.
(2) There is a danger of gender discrimination resulting from a finding of special financial contribution, because it is harder for a home-maker to demonstrate.
(3) There might be cases where the product alone justified a conclusion of special contribution, but absent some exceptional and individual quality in the generator of the fortune, a case for special contribution must be hard to establish.
(4) The concept of exceeded expectations as the test for special contribution was rejected.
(5) A finding of equality of contribution may be followed by an order for unequal division because of the influence of one or more of the other statutory criteria as well as the over-arching search for fairness

HC **_Norris v Norris_ [2003] 1 FLR 1142**

The wife claimed more than half the entire matrimonial assets, primarily because of her exceptional financial contribution to the marriage, in the form of her inherited property which had been used to support the husband's company during difficult times. The husband had repaid all the money loaned, with interest.

The use of 'exceptional contribution' to give a spouse a share greater than equality of division would happen only in very limited and quite exceptional circumstances.

HC *Sorrell v Sorrell* [2005] EWHC 1717 (Fam)

The assets of the marriage were £75 million. The husband argued that his taking a small company to become the second largest of its kind in the world was a special contribution which justified a departure from equality. Further, the shares he held should be discounted because if he as a 'key man' in the business left, the shares would be devalued.

A departure from equality was justified by the husband's special contribution to the marriage, in the form of exceptional business talent amounting to genius. The court had to make a broad-brush appraisal based on the evidence, and on that basis the husband had established that he was regarded within the wider business community as a most exceptional and talented businessmen. No share discount was given because there was no indication that the husband was planning to leave the business. He received 60 per cent of the assets.

3.6 Dealing with inheritances

HC *MT v MT (Financial Provision: Lump Sum)* [1992] 1 FLR 362

The husband was due to inherit from his father, who was a wealthy 83-year-old. Under German law he could not be disinherited and would get an eighth of the estate. There was a marital debt secured on this anticipated inheritance. The wife said that there should be an adjournment of the ancillary relief to allow consideration of the inheritance.

On an application for a lump sum in circumstances where there was a real possibility of capital from a specific source becoming available in the near future, and where an order for an adjournment was the only means whereby justice could be done to the parties, there was a discretionary jurisdiction to order an adjournment of the application.

HC *D v D (Lump Sum Order: Adjournment of Application)* [2001] 1 FLR 633

At the time of the final ancillary relief hearing, the husband was due a bonus of an unspecified amount under a bonus scheme. The wife's lump sum claim was adjourned pending quantification of the claim. The husband appealed.

It is rare to adjourn part of a claim, and that should only be done if there is a real possibility of capital from a specific source becoming available in the near future. Here it was correct, as justice would not have been done to this wife if the district judge had dismissed her lump sum claim, and justice would not have been done to the husband if a lump sum order had been made against him before the court knew what, if any, bonus payment he would receive.

HC *Norris v Norris* [2003] 1 FLR 1142

The wife had contributed inherited property which had been used to support the husband's company during difficult times. The husband had repaid all the money loaned, with interest.

Inherited assets should not be quarantined from the pool of assets. The mere fact that inherited property had not been touched or had not become part of the matrimonial pot was not necessarily, without more, a reason for excluding it from the court's discretionary exercise. Inherited property represented a contribution made to the welfare of the family by one of the parties, and was one of the factors to be taken into account.

HL *White v White* [2000] 2 FLR 981

Lord Nicholls

'[An inheritance] represents a contribution made to the welfare of the family by one of the parties to the marriage. The judge should take it into account. He should decide how important it is in the particular case. The nature and value of the property, and the time when and circumstances in which the property was acquired, are among the relevant matters to be considered. However, in the ordinary course, this factor can be expected to carry little weight, if any, in a case where the claimant's financial needs cannot be met without recourse to this property.'

CA *P v P (Inherited Property)* [2004] EWCA Civ 1364

The assets included a farm handed down through generations of the husband's family.

Fairness might require quite a different approach if the inheritance was a pecuniary legacy that accrued during the marriage than if the inheritance were a landed estate that had been within one spouse's family for generations and had been brought into the marriage with an expectation that it would be retained in specie for future generations. On the facts it was fair that the wife got a needs-based award.

3.7 Short marriages

CA *H v H (Financial Provision: Short Marriage)* (1981) 2 FLR 392

Balcombe LJ

'[With] short marriage[s] between two young persons, neither of whom has been adversely affected financially by the consequences of the marriage and [where] each . . . is fully capable of earning his or her own living, the approach which the court should normally adopt is to allow for a short period of periodical payments to allow the party . . . in the weaker financial position . . . to adjust herself to the situation, and thereafter to achieve the wholly desirable result of a clean break.'

CA *Foster v Foster* [2003] 2 FLR 299

In a four-year marriage, to which the wife brought more capital and had a higher income, the couple made a substantial sum of money dealing with property.

It was appropriate to return to the parties the capital they had and to spilt the profit equally between them. The higher income did not justify a higher capital split.

HL *Miller v Miller* [2006] UKHL 24; [2006] 1 FLR 1186

Mr Miller, a multi-millionaire, left his wife for another woman after less than three years' marriage. The wife had little capital. At first instance Singer J said that although the wife did not raise conduct under s 25(2)(g) MCA 1973, it was relevant for him to consider the reason for the breakdown of the marriage. He awarded Mrs Miller £5 million, on the basis that she expected to be married to a wealthy man for a long time. The husband had £17.5 million, plus shares valued at between £12 and £18 million. The Court of Appeal upheld the decision. The husband appealed, arguing that the reason for the breakdown was irrelevant and that in a short marriage the parties should be returned to the position they were in before the marriage.

(1) Standard of living is a relevant factor, but hopes and expectations as such are not an appropriate basis on which to assess financial needs. Claims for expectation losses do not sit comfortably with the notion that each party is free to end the marriage.

(2) It is incorrect that one cannot be 'fair' without knowing the reason for the breakdown of the marriage. It is only conduct which is inequitable to disregard that must be taken into account.

(3) Property is divided into marital acquest property – gained by the parties by their own efforts during the marriage – and non-marital acquest property – e.g. inheritance, pre-owned property. The former is available to be shared fairly in all cases, the latter is shared only if it is fair to do so on the particular facts of the case.

(4) The House of Lords also awarded Mrs Miller £5 million, but on the basis that it was fair to give her a one-third share of the assets accumulated during the marriage because much of the effort which had resulted in their accumulation had been pre-marriage.

3.8 Loss of high earnings

CA *McFarlane v McFarlane; Parlour v Parlour* [2004] 2 FLR 893

Both wives sought periodical payments for sums greater than their needs. Mr McFarlane was a successful accountant who would continue to earn for years to come at a high level. Mr Parlour was a professional footballer whose large income was likely to decrease dramatically once his contract ended. Both wives said that their contributions to their husband's careers meant that it was fair for them to have a large share of future income. Capital division was agreed.

The court did have power to order periodical payments in excess of needs. In exceptional cases term orders could be used to allow the recipient to accumulate capital. The court had to consider the possibility of a subsequent clean break, particularly where there was a surplus of income over needs that could found the basis of a clean break, even though there was insufficient capital to achieve that now.

The recipient must invest the surplus sensibly. The saving up for a clean break should be done within five years. Term maintenance orders were made at sums greater than needs.

HL *McFarlane v McFarlane* [2006] UKHL 24; [2006] 1 FLR 1186

See notes on general principles from the case above.

Mrs McFarlane appealed from the Court of Appeal. Mrs Parlour did not.

This was a future clean break case, but it was fairer to expect the husband to return to court to achieve it than expect the wife to save up. If some of her periodical payments were to compensate for loss of her own income, it was not fair that she should have to accumulate capital from it. She got a joint life order for more than her income needs.

Mrs Parlour's case was different from Mrs McFarlane's, in that she did not in fact give up a good job for marriage and to care for children.

3.9 Liquidity

CA *Wells v Wells* [2002] 2 FLR 97

Because of its precarious trading position, the husband's business could not be properly valued. The court awarded the majority of the other realisable assets to the wife and left the husband with the business.

It was wrong to leave the wife the bulk of those assets which were readily saleable at stable prices, and the husband all those assets which were substantially more illiquid and risk-laden.

The wife should have been given an increased shareholding in the business and the husband the ready assets, so that the parties shared in the advantages and disadvantages of the family business.

3.10 Pensions

T v T (Financial Relief: Pensions) [1998] 1 FLR 1073

The wife sought a pension earmarking order against the husband's pension, arguing that she was entitled to such an order, which should last for her lifetime.

There was no right to compensation for pension loss. The court must consider lump sums and/or periodical payments then consider if the pension position should alter those orders which it might not. Any order for earmarked income was akin to periodical payments and would end on the wife's remarriage and be subject to variation. It was hard to predict far into the future sums that would be paid as a result of earmarking, and it might be better to do that once the husband had retired by way of variation of maintenance. Earmarking of the death in service benefit could be used to protect the wife from loss of periodical payments in the event of the husband's death.

Burrow v Burrow [1999] 1 FLR 508

An order earmarking 50 per cent of capital and 50 per cent of income from a pension scheme was made. The husband appealed.

The law remained discretionary and did not require a mathematical or arithmetical compensation of lost pension benefits to which a party might otherwise claim an entitlement. For income, the correct approach was to determine income requirements in the usual way, rather than divide equally. Different considerations applied to the capital which would not be lost on remarriage and an equal division could reflect the contributions to the marriage even though it would not be available for some years.

CA *Maskell v Maskell* [2003] 1 FLR 1138

The wife was given the home with equity of £26,000 and a policy of £6,000. The 41-year-old husband retained a policy of £4,000 and a pension of £32,000.

The husband was given leave to appeal out of time. There was a fundamental flaw in the judge's approach, because he had made the seemingly elementary mistake of confusing present capital with a right to financial benefits on retirement, only 25 per cent of which maximum could be taken in capital terms, the other 75 per cent being taken as an annuity stream. He had simply failed to compare like with like. The prospect of the husband, at 41 years of age, receiving either capital or income from the pension fund was deferred, if not distant, and there was a fundamental anxiety that there had been an injustice in this case.

HC *R (Smith) v Secretary of State for Defence and Secretary of State for Work and Pensions* [2005] 1 FLR 97

A 56-year-old wife obtained a pension share. The husband (59), a retired army general, had a pension in payment. When the order was implemented his income was halved but no payments were to be made to the wife until she was 60, the normal retirement age of the scheme. The wife argued that she was being discriminated against, contrary to the European Convention for the Protection of Human Rights and Fundamental Freedoms 1950.

The provision differentiated not only directly on grounds of age, but also indirectly on grounds of gender when it delayed payment to the pension credit member until the age of 60, even in circumstances in which the active member was receiving or would receive his pension prior to the age of 60. The circumstances of the female beneficiary of a pension-sharing order and of her ex-husband were sufficiently similar as to call, in the mind of a rational and fair-minded person, for a positive justification for the different and ostensibly prejudicial treatment of the woman in comparison with the man. The justification for the differentiation was that it encouraged ex-wives under the age of 60 to work until that age. Encouragement to ex-spouses to work until the age of 60 was a legitimate aim of the state, and the provision was a proportionate response to that aim. If an ex-spouse could not support herself until 60, then the remedy was a maintenance order.

The wife intends to take this to the European Court of Human Rights.

3.11 Conduct

 HC *Al-Kahatib v Masry* [2002] 1 FLR 1053

The husband, a Saudi, refused to co-operate with the process at all and abducted the children to Saudi Arabia. The wife asserted he was worth $200 million, the husband asserted he was insolvent. The court found that he had hidden assets all around the world and that it could not accept as the truth anything the husband said unless it was either an admission or otherwise contrary to his interests.

The husband was found guilty of serious and persistent misconduct. The court was entitled to draw the inference that he had sufficient assets to satisfy the wife's claim and that the £23 million she got was not more than one-half of the family assets.

The wife was also given an additional £2,500,000 to fight the abduction of the children to Saudi Arabia. If he returned the children, the excess money not spent on legal fees should be returned to the husband.

HC *H v H (Financial Relief: Attempted Murder as Conduct)* [2005] EWHC 2911 (Fam)

The husband was convicted of attempting to murder his wife and sentenced to 12 years' imprisonment. The wife was deeply traumatised and unable to continue with her career in the police. The children saw the attack. She was likely to receive an award under the criminal injuries compensation scheme of about £100,000.

(1) Conduct like this colours the court's approach to its consideration of the other party in s 25(2) MCA 1973 factors, especially the needs of the parties. The court should not be punitive or confiscatory for its own sake. Conduct is treated as a potentially magnifying factor when considering the other subsections and criteria. It places the wife's needs as a much higher priority to those of the husband.

(2) The effects of the conduct must be taken into account. The wife's mental health was affected. She could no longer remain in the matrimonial home, where the attack had taken place. Much of her earning capacity had been destroyed. The children were likely to be affected by what they had witnessed. The husband would be making no contribution, either financially or to the upbringing of the children. His behaviour was likely to affect the wife's relationship with a new partner.

(3) It was fair that the wife got far more than the husband.

HC **McMinn v McMinn (Ancillary Relief: Death of Party to Proceedings: Costs)** [2003] 2 FLR 839

An ancillary relief order gave the wife a lump sum of £75,000, but before implementation or decree absolute, the husband stabbed the wife to death. Her executors sought to enforce the order and failed because under s 23(5) no cause of action survived death. They sought their costs of the proceedings.

The executors failed, but were entirely reasonable in bringing the application. Success is a very material factor in determining costs. Conduct extraneous to the proceedings would not normally be relevant to costs, but here it would be artificial to ignore the murder. The furthest the court could go was to make no order for costs.

3.12 Cohabitation before marriage

HC *Co v Co* [2004] 1 FLR 1095

The parties lived together for six years, having two children, then were married for four years.

To reflect society's changing values, periods of cohabitation leading seamlessly to marriage should be counted as part of the marriage and count towards its length.

3.13 Cohabitation after marriage

HC *Kimber v Kimber* [2000] 1 FLR 383

The husband was to pay spousal maintenance until the wife cohabited for three months. A man moved in with her, then moved out when the husband ceased the maintenance.

It was impossible to draw up an exhaustive definition of cohabitation, but the following factors are relevant:

- The parties were living together in the same household and the living together involved a sharing of daily tasks and duties.
- There was stability and permanence in the relationship.
- The financial affairs of the couple were indicative of their relationship.
- Their sexual relationship was admitted and ongoing.
- There was a close bond between the wife's new partner and the wife's child.
- As regards the motives of the couple, it was clear that the wife had denied cohabitation so as to continue to enjoy the payment of maintenance from her husband.
- There was sufficient evidence that cohabitation existed in the opinion of a reasonable person with normal perceptions.

3.14 Housing

HL *Piglowska v Piglowska* [1999] 2 FLR 763

The case turned around the parties' housing needs. The wife wished to retain the matrimonial home, worth £100,000. Total assets were £124,000. The husband said it should be sold and the assets divided so he and his new wife could return from Poland and also buy in the UK. Costs were high, meaning that a modest award to the husband would be eaten up by the statutory charge to the (then) Legal Aid Board. The wife was given the house.

The wife retained the house. There was no rule that spouses' housing needs were to be given greater weight than the other criteria listed in s 25. The effect of the Legal Aid charge does not justify a greater award to one party.

In cases where there are minor children, their needs for housing may well require their carer to be housed. However, housing can be achieved in rented property.

3.15 Prenuptial contracts

HC *M v M (Prenuptial Agreement)* [2002] FLR 654

The parties entered into a prenuptial agreement in Canada. The husband had been divorced and was not prepared to remarry without a contract. The wife got legal advice that it was against her interest, but signed because she was pregnant and wanted to be married. The husband was worth around £7.5 million. The contract said that the wife was to receive £275,000. She claimed £1.3 million, saying she had been pressurised into the contract. The husband was ordered to pay £875,000 on a clean-break basis and £15,000 for child maintenance plus school fees.

Under s 25 the court's overriding duty was to arrive at a solution that was fair in all the circumstances. The first consideration was the child's welfare. It was in her interest to reside with her mother and to have a period of security. It was reasonable for the mother to reside in England. The court was required to have regard to all the circumstances of the case. The prenuptial agreement was relevant, either as part of the circumstances or as conduct under s 25(2)(g). The court's duty was to look at the agreement and decide, in the particular circumstances, what weight should in justice be given to it. In this case it would be unjust to the husband to ignore its existence and terms.

HC *K v K (Ancillary Relief: Prenuptial Agreement)* [2003] 1 FLR 120

The husband and wife with one child separated after 14 months. The agreement said she should have a £100,000 lump sum plus 10 per cent per year of marriage and reasonable provision for the child. On divorce, she sought £1.6 million and periodic payments of £57,000 for herself and £15,000 for the child p.a. The husband offered £600,000 in trust for the child to buy a house plus a £120,000 lump sum for the wife.

There were no grounds for saying this agreement would lead to an injustice if it were upheld. It was conduct that it would be inequitable to disregard. The wife should have £120,000 and her claims dismissed. The agreement was silent on maintenance. She had to invest time in bringing up the child and based on her earning capacity it would be unjust to the wife not to give her maintenance, even if the agreement precluded such a claim. She should get £15,000 (on top of her own income of £40–50,000). A child of parents between whom there was a great disparity of wealth was entitled to be brought up in circumstances which bore some kind of relationship to the standards of living of the wealthier parent.

The husband should pay £1.2 million to provide a home and furniture for the wife until the child ceased to be in full-time education, at which time the capital should revert to the husband.

HC *J v J (Disclosure: Offshore Corporations)* [2004] 1 FLR 1042

There had been a prenuptial contract in this case by which the wife relinquished all claims to the husband's interest in the family business.

It was held to be of no significance. It was signed on the eve of marriage with no disclosure and no legal advice. It did not make provision for the arrival of children.

3.16 Post-separation agreements

CA *Edgar v Edgar* (1980) 2 FLR 19

A wife of a multi-millionaire entered into a separation deed which gave her some capital provision and contained a clause stating that she would not seek further provision after divorce. Later she issued ancillary relief proceedings. The husband argued that she should be bound by the undertaking in the agreement.

(1) There was jurisdiction to consider the wife's claim despite the undertaking.
(2) Such an agreement came under the heading of 'conduct' and should be considered in all the circumstances.

> (3) Reasons not to uphold an agreement might include undue pressure, exploitation of a dominant position, inadequate knowledge, possibly bad legal advice, or an important change of circumstances.
>
> (4) It was important that formal agreements, properly and fairly arrived at with competent legal advice, should not be displaced unless there were good and substantial grounds for concluding that an injustice would be done by holding the parties to the terms of their agreement.

HC *X v X (Y intervening)* **[2002] 1 FLR 508**

The parties were Jewish. When the marriage broke down the wife's family agreed to give the husband £500,000 if he gave her a religious divorce. The district judge was told that the husband had £600,000 and a high income. The wife had no means whatsoever. The DJ refused to make the consent order. The wife refused to take any further steps to convert the agreement into an order. The husband made an application for the wife to show cause why the agreement should not be made an order.

(1) The wife should be held to an agreement, which she had entered into after the most expert legal advice and where there was no undue pressure.

(2) The fact that one party might have done better by going to court is not a ground to allow them to resile from the agreement.

(3) The circumstances are to be regarded in their totality and with a broad perspective, rather than individually one-by-one.

(4) The relevant circumstances are not limited to the purely financial aspects of the agreement; social, personal, religious and cultural considerations all have to be taken into account.

3.17 Third party interests in property

CA *Thomas v Thomas* [1995] 2 FLR 668

Where a spouse enjoyed access to wealth, but no absolute entitlement to it, the court would not act in direct invasion of the rights of a third party, nor put a third party under pressure to act in a way which would enhance the means of the maintaining spouse, but nevertheless need not act in total disregard of the potential availability of wealth from sources owned or administered by others.

HC *TL v ML and Others (Ancillary Relief: Claim Against Assets of Extended Family)* [2005] EWHC 2860 (Fam), [2006] 1 FLR 1263

Where a dispute arose in financial relief proceedings about the ownership of property which involved a third party, the third party must be joined to the proceedings at the earliest opportunity, directions should be given for the issue to be fully pleaded by points of claim and points of defence, separate witness statements should be filed in relation to the dispute and the dispute should be heard separately as a preliminary issue before the financial dispute resolution hearing. The principles of law on property ownership are the same as in the Chancery division.

3.18 Interim maintenance

A v A (Maintenance Pending Suit: Provision for Legal Fees)
[2001] 1 FLR 377 HC

The wife obtained a maintenance pending suit order which rendered her ineligible for public funding of her costs. She applied for an upward variation.

Maintenance payments under s 22 MCA 1973 were not restricted to matters of daily living in its most literal and restrictive sense, and legal fees incurred in the course of litigation were recurrent expenses of an income nature which could be covered by a maintenance pending suit order. It was reasonable provision to enable the wife to progress her claim.

Moses-Taiga v Taiga [2005] EWCA Civ 1013

The wife claimed a customary Nigerian marriage and jurisdiction to divorce in the UK based on habitual residence. The husband denied both. The wife applied for maintenance pending suit to include an element for legal costs.

The court had jurisdiction to grant maintenance pending suit under s 22 of the Matrimonial Causes Act 1973, even if the respondent had challenged the court's jurisdiction for any reason. Section 22 MCA 1973 allowed an element for legal fees in an MPS order if an applicant had no assets, no security for borrowings and could not persuade her solicitors to enter into a charge on assets the applicant was anticipated to gain at the end of the case.

CA *Currey v Currey* [2006] EWCA Civ 1338

Even if the applicant satisfies the criteria in *Moses-Taiga*, other factors may lead the court to decline an element of legal costs in an MPS order. The subject matter of the application and the reasonableness of the applicant's stance will be important. An award should be made only until the financial dispute resolution hearing and then a different judge should consider its extension.

3.19 Interim lump sums

HC *Barry v Barry* [1992] 2 FLR 233

The former matrimonial home was sold and the proceeds held by solicitors pending a final hearing. The wife was anxious to buy a property, on which she would have to complete before the hearing, and sought release of some of the sale proceeds to fund the purchase. She acknowledged that the new house would still be part of the 'pot' of assets available for distribution at the final hearing. The husband opposed the money being made illiquid.

While a hearing was pending there was jurisdiction to allocate a particular asset to satisfy the contingent and unadjudicated claim of a party, subject to any necessary undertakings or conditions. In each case the question should be posed whether the proposed substitution of assets threatened to place a fetter on the dispositive powers of the judge at that hearing, and, if it did, whether the threat was justifiable on overriding grounds of individual or family welfare.

CA *Wicks v Wicks* [1998] 1 FLR 470

The wife sought a lump sum from sale proceeds of a house on an interim basis pending final hearing. At first instance the court considered *Barry v Barry* and concluded that there was jurisdiction to make an interim lump sum. The husband appealed, challenging that jurisdiction.

There was no statutory power to make an interim lump sum. And (even if such a power had existed) there was no power to make an order for the application of the proceeds of sale in the exercise of an inherent jurisdiction. *Barry v Barry* was disapproved. The inherent jurisdiction of the court did not confer a general residual discretion to make any order necessary to ensure that justice be done between the parties.

HC *Re G (Maintenance Pending Suit)* [2006] EWHC 1834 (Fam)

A mother sought, alongside interim maintenance, a sum to pay for her son's bar mitzvah celebrations.

There is no power to order an interim lump sum but, where the money is for the benefit of the child, Sch 1 CA 1989

allows such a lump sum. The wife obtained £46,000 for the party!

3.20 Term maintenance

CA *Jones v Jones* [2000] 2 FLR 307

The husband was subject to an order for term maintenance which ran out on 12th January 1998. The wife issued an application to extend the term on 8th January 1998. At the hearing (after 12th January) the husband argued that there were now no periodical payments to extend.

There is power to vary a term maintenance order as long as the application is issued before the term expires.

3.21 Mesher orders

CA *Dorney Kingdom v Dorney Kingdom* [2000] 2 FLR 855

A husband obtained a Mesher order at a lower percentage than he had hoped.

Thorpe J

'The court is not empowered to redraw the boundary between the respective beneficial interests of the parties at will. A respondent's beneficial interest shall only be reduced or settled in so far as the reasonable requirements of the applicant and the children necessitate.'

When deciding the percentage, the court must consider the cost of rehousing the spouse remaining in the home and the cost to her of maintaining the house in the meantime.

CA *Elliot v Elliot* [2001] 1 FCR 477

A Mesher order is a way to avoid gender discrimination. As soon as the wife's responsibilities as home-maker for the children reach a point of natural termination, the husband is entitled to his capital share.

HC *B v B (Mesher Order)* [2002] EWHC 3106 (Fam)

The wife obtained an outright lump sum. The husband claimed it should be a Mesher order.

The court must look at the fairness of the order, both now and when it is implemented in the future. An outright lump sum was correct because a Mesher order would confer a slight advantage on the husband but cause the wife a significant disadvantage in the future.

CHAPTER 4

CHILD MAINTENANCE AND SCHEDULE 1 CHILDREN ACT 1989

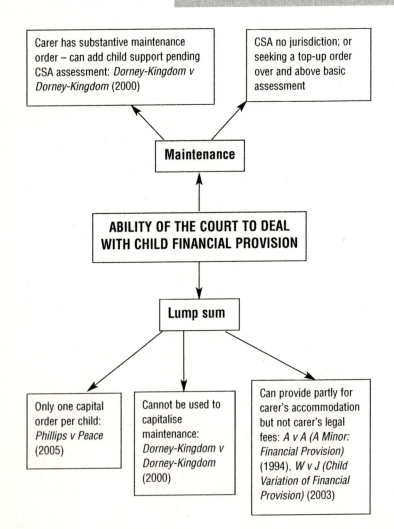

Carer has substantive maintenance order – can add child support pending CSA assessment: *Dorney-Kingdom v Dorney-Kingdom* (2000)

CSA no jurisdiction; or seeking a top-up order over and above basic assessment

Maintenance

ABILITY OF THE COURT TO DEAL WITH CHILD FINANCIAL PROVISION

Lump sum

Only one capital order per child: *Phillips v Peace* (2005)

Cannot be used to capitalise maintenance: *Dorney-Kingdom v Dorney-Kingdom* (2000)

Can provide partly for carer's accommodation but not carer's legal fees: *A v A (A Minor: Financial Provision)* (1994), *W v J (Child Variation of Financial Provision)* (2003)

4.1 Court orders

 CA *Dorney-Kingdom v Dorney-Kingdom* [2000] 2 FLR 855

The wife had only an entitlement to nominal maintenance for herself. The husband did not agree a sum for child maintenance and the CSA had not yet made its assessment. He claimed that the court had no jurisdiction to order any child maintenance pending CSA assessment

The court had no jurisdiction to make an order for periodical payments to children where the wife had only a nominal claim to support, unless the parties consented. Although an order for spousal maintenance (a so-called 'Segal order') under s 23 Matrimonial Causes Act 1973 could incorporate some of the costs of supporting children, which would reduce *pro tanto* from the date upon which the Child Support Agency brings in an assessment, any such order had to include a substantial ingredient of spousal support to be legitimate.

4.2 Interplay with the CSA

HC *Phillips v Peace* [1996] 2 FLR 230

The CSA assessed a father as having no income and thus not being liable for child support. He did have substantial capital assets and a company. The mother of his child sought a lump sum to be used to provide regular support for the child.

If the CSA had jurisdiction to make an assessment the court still retained its jurisdiction under s 15 of the Children Act 1989 to make orders for the transfer and settlement of property. However the court should do so only in order to meet the need of the child in respect of a particular item of capital expenditure. He was ordered to provide a house for the child.

4.3 Limit of one capital order

HC *Phillips v Peace* [2005] 2 FLR 1212

The mother sought further capital provision for housing, stating that the original house, provided in 1996, was now too small for the child and her sibling (born to an unknown father). Other capital claims were also made.

The prohibition in para 1(5)(b) on the making of 'more than one order [requiring the settlement of property or requiring the transfer of property] against the same person in respect of the same child' should be read conjunctively rather than disjunctively, so that if either form of property adjustment order, settlement of property or transfer of property, had been made, no further order adjusting property rights could be made. Nor was there a power to review or to vary a property adjustment order of either sort, or to vary any lump sum order (except for a lump sum by instalments).

4.4 Carer's allowance

A v A (A Minor: Financial Provision) [1994] 1 FLR 657

The father had bought a house in which the mother and his child had lived for some time. The mother sought an outright transfer of that property to her for the benefit of the child, or to the child.

Property adjustment orders should not ordinarily be made to provide benefits for the child after he or she has attained independence. The proper order was for a settlement of the property for the benefit of the child while she was under the control of her mother, the mother would have a right to occupy the property to the exclusion of the father and without paying rent for the purpose of looking after the child.

4.5 Levels of maintenance

Re P (A Child: Financial Provision) [2003] EWCA Civ 837

A mother applied for provision for her child from a multi-millionaire. The High Court had been concerned to ensure that the provision was not provision for an unmarried partner by the back door.

The mother's entitlement to an allowance as the primary carer should be checked but not diminished by the absence of any direct claim in law. The court should recognise the responsibility, and often sacrifice, of the unmarried parent (generally the mother) who was to be the primary carer of the child. The carer should have control of a budget that reflects her position and that of the father, both social and financial. The mother was accordingly awarded a housing fund of £1 million, £100,000 for internal decoration and periodical payments of £70,000 per annum (less state benefits).

4.6 Welfare of the child

HC ***W v J (Child: Variation of Financial Provision)*** **[2003] EWHC 2657 (Fam)**

An unmarried American mother sought an increase in the periodical payments she was receiving for her child, such increase to include an element for her legal fees in regard to further litigation about the child.

There is no jurisdiction to use Sch I Children Act 1989 to make a payment to cover legal fees. Payments have to be for the benefit of the child, and legal fees were for the benefit of the parent not the child. Nor can the inherent jurisdiction be used to achieve the same aim.

CHAPTER 5

DOMESTIC VIOLENCE AND HARASSMENT

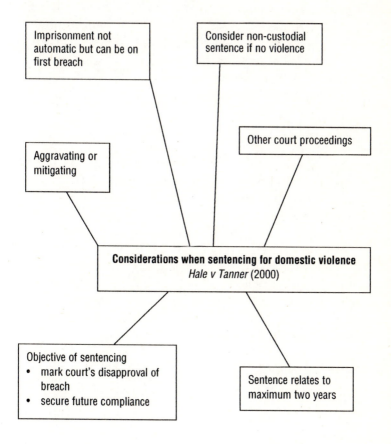

Imprisonment not automatic but can be on first breach

Consider non-custodial sentence if no violence

Other court proceedings

Aggravating or mitigating

Considerations when sentencing for domestic violence
Hale v Tanner (2000)

Objective of sentencing
- mark court's disapproval of breach
- secure future compliance

Sentence relates to maximum two years

5.1 Scope of occupation orders

HC *S v F (Occupation Order)* [2002] 1 FLR 255

The father had remarried, with four children, and lived in Malaysia. The wife remained in London. When she decided to move to the country the son of her marriage refused to go. The mother left anyway, leaving the boy in London. The father applied for an occupation order allowing him to return to the matrimonial home and care for his son there.

Despite the fact that there had been no violence, an occupation order was granted. Applying s 35(6) FLA 1996 the court balanced the facts that the father's financial position was far graver than the mother's. An order might lead to some financial inconvenience for the mother, whereas it would provide essential security for the son and the rest of the family. The mother's sudden change of plan for her children and her failure to consult the father adequately or in time made her partly responsible at least for the son's intransigence. The period of the parties' separation, though long, had to be seen in the context of a continuing parental responsibility.

CA *Chalmers v Johns* [1999] 1 FLR 392

The police had been called four times when the spouses had inflicted minor injuries on each other. The father often took the seven-year-old daughter to her school near the home. The judge made an occupation order in favour of the mother, allowing her to return to the property and ousting the father.

Under s 33 FLA 1996, the court first must apply s 33(7) if there is a risk of significant harm if an order is not made. If there is such risk, then an order is mandatory, unless the risk to the respondent or child would be the same or higher if an order were made. If there is no such risk then the discretionary factors in s 33(6) are applied. Occupation orders are for exceptional circumstances. Inconveniences of a longer journey to school do not suffice.

CA *B v B (Occupation Order)* [1999] Fam Law 208

The mother left the father because of violence by him, and was housed with their baby in unsuitable bed and breakfast accommodation. The father had living with him a child of a previous relationship aged six. The council said that they would not rehouse him, because he would be intentionally homeless. The judge made an occupation order in favour of the mother.

On appeal the order was overturned. The judge had failed to assess correctly the risk of significant harm that would be caused to the six-year-old, who would have to live in homeless accommodation and move school or else be taken into care by the social services. The mother would in a matter of weeks be moved to better accommodation as she was in priority need.

This case turned on its facts and the housing policy was an important factor. The court stressed that the fact that a father has a residence order for children of the family should not normally prevent occupation orders being made against them.

5.2 Sentencing

CA *Hale v Tanner* [2000] 2 FLR 879

Family sentencing for contempt was different to criminal sentencing, and no guidelines for appropriate sentences after a breach of a non-molestation order or occupation order could be given, but the following guidelines were set out:

(1) Imprisonment is not an automatic response to the breach of an order, but there is no principle that imprisonment was not to be imposed on the first occasion.

(2) Non-custodial sentences should be considered, in particular where no violence was involved.

(3) If imprisonment was appropriate, the length of the committal should be decided without reference to whether or not it was to be suspended.

(4) The seriousness of the contempt had to be judged not only for its intrinsic gravity but also in the light of the court's objectives, both to mark its disapproval of the disobedience to the order and to secure compliance in the future.

(5) The length of the committal should relate to the maximum available, i.e. two years.

(6) Suspension was possible in a wider range of circumstances than in criminal cases, and was usually the first way of attempting to secure compliance with the order.

(7) The court had to consider whether the context was mitigating or aggravating, in particular where there was a breach of an intimate relationship and/or children were involved.

(8) The court should consider any concurrent proceedings in another court, and should explain to the contemnor the nature of the order and the consequence of breach.

QBD *DPP v Tweddell* [2002] 2 FLR 40

The husband was sentenced to contempt of court for breach of a non-molestation order and later prosecuted for the same facts. He complained that the prosecution was an abuse of process, as he would be punished twice for one offence.

Contempt proceedings and criminal proceedings had different purposes. Contempt proceedings mark the court's disapproval of disobedience of its order, and aim to secure future compliance with the order. Criminal proceedings protect the public order by punishing offenders in order to protect the public and providing a deterrence.

The civil and the criminal courts should take into account any punishment previously imposed on the individual by another court in respect of an incident when deciding itself what penalty to impose in respect of the same incident.

CA *Nwogbe v Nwogbe* [2000] 2 FLR 44

An occupation order was made against Mr Nwogbe and an order under s 40 FLA 1996 that he pay rent and certain bills. He failed to pay and the wife attempted to have him committed to prison.

A s 40 FLA 1996 order can be made but there is no power to commit for breach of them because of the application of s 4 of the Debtors Act 1869, which abolished arrest or imprisonment for default in payment, as modified by the Administration of Justice Act 1970.

5.3 Protection from Harassment Act 1997

QBD *Lau v DPP* [2000] I FLR 799

Five incidents of harassment were alleged in a prosecution under the PHA 1997. The magistrates found only two to be founded, those events being four months apart. The defendant was convicted.

Only two incidents are needed for 'a course of conduct', but the fewer the occasions and the further spread apart they are, the less likely a finding of harassment can be made.

CA *R v Hills* [2001] 1 FLR 580

There was evidence of assaults in April and October with hair pulling in-between. The parties had been reconciling and having sexual intercourse between incidents. The defendant was convicted of harassment.

On appeal the conviction was quashed. Harassment was a particular and discrete offence, and required a course of conduct. While two incidents distanced in time could constitute a course of conduct, it was necessary to find cogent linking conduct between them in order for a course of conduct to be proved. The state of affairs was far from the 'stalking' type of offence for which the 1997 Act was intended.

CC *Gina Satvir Singh v (1) Prithvipal Singh Bhakar (2) Dalbir Kaur Bhakar* [2007] 1 FLR 830

A young Sikh woman was subjected to abuse by her mother-in-law, with whom she lived. The abuse included making her cut her hair and wearing a locket with Hindu symbols, both of which were religiously offensive to her. As a result of the abuse the claimant suffered a psychiatric condition. She issued a free-standing claim for damages under s 3 PHA 1997.

There is nothing to prevent family members from using the PHA 1997. Damages of £35,000 were awarded. This was at the top end of the recommended rate for psychiatric injury because, unlike in a road traffic accident, this was not purely compensation for injury flowing from a one-off incident but also compensation for the months of abuse suffered leading to the ongoing injury.

CHAPTER 6

INTRODUCTION TO THE CHILDREN ACT 1989

BASIC PRINCIPLES OF THE CHILDREN ACT

Paramountcy principle

- In conflict between children choose the lesser of two evils: *Re A (Children) (Conjoined Twins: Surgical Separation)* (2000)
- It is the welfare of the child who is subject of the application that is paramount: *F v Leeds City Council* (1994)

No-order principle

- No factors exist that create a presumption in favour of a court order. The burden is on the applicant to make a positive case for an order: *Re X and Y (Leave to Remove from the Jurisdiction) (No Order Principle)* (2001)

Welfare checklist

- There is a strong supposition the child should be with natural biological parents: *Re W (A Minor) (Residence Order)* (1993), *Re G (Children)* (2006)
- Childrens views are usually taken indirectly but should be respected: *Re M (Family Proceedings: Affidavits)* (1995), *Re S (Contact) (Children's Views)* (2002)
- Siblings should be together: *C v C (Minors) (Custody)* (1988)
- No presumption in favour of mothers over fathers: *Re W (A Minor) (Residence Order)* (1992)
- Religion is only one of the factors but children should continue to be exposed to any dual heritages: *Re P (Section 91 (14) Guidelines) (Residence and Religious Heritage)* (1999), *Re S (Specific Issue Order: Religion: Circumcision)* (2005)
- Welfare of the child comes before religious freedom of adults: *Haringey London Borough Council v C (E, E, F and High Commissioner of Republic of Kenya Intervening)* (2007)
- Continuity of care is important: *Diocco v Milne* (1983)

Standard of proof

Balance of probabilities based on proven facts not mere suspicion: *Re M and R (Child Abuse: Evidence)* (1996)

6.1 Operating the section 1 principles

CA *Re A (Children) (Conjoined Twins: Surgical Separation)*
[2000] 4 All ER 961 CA

J and M were conjoined twins, joined at the abdomen. J could live independently but separation would result in the death of M. If there was no operation both would die within 3–6 months because M was in effect draining the blood from J. The hospital obtained a declaration that they should perform the operation. The parents appealed.

The question was whether it was in M's best interests that the operation be performed, which it was not. Looking at her position in isolation the court should not sanction the operation. However given the conflict of interest and the need to give paramountcy to the interest of each twin, the court had to choose the lesser of two evils and find the least detrimental alternative. The balance came down heavily in favour of J.

CA *F v Leeds City Council* [1994] 2 FLR 60

A 15-year-old being held in secure accommodation under a care order became pregnant. The baby was taken into care. The mother appealed, saying that the baby's welfare should not alone have been the paramount consideration as the mother was herself still a minor.

In determining whether the welfare of the infant or that of the child-parent was paramount, the correct approach was to identify which child was the subject of the application, and which child it was whose welfare was directly involved.

6.2 Purposive delay

HC *Re B (A Minor) (Contact) (Interim Order)* [1994] 2 FLR 269

Parents agreed before magistrates that although the matter was listed for a final hearing, there should be an interim contact order to the father, who would see the child in a contact centre with the court welfare officer observing two sessions and a review in four months' time. The bench refused to do this, saying it would be against the principle of no delay.

Section 1(2) of the Children Act 1989 set out the principle that delay in determining any question with respect to the upbringing of a child was likely to prejudice the welfare of the child. A proposal that there should be a monitored programme of contact could not be regarded as being detrimental to a child. The result of the magistrates' decision was that the child was being deprived of the possible benefit of seeing her father for four months.

6.3 No-order principle

HC *Re X and Y (Leave to Remove from the Jurisdiction) (No-Order Principle)* [2001] 2 FLR 1156

The mother obtained leave to remove the children from the jurisdiction. The father argued that the court had failed to take into account the no-order principle.

The party applying for an order had the burden of making out a positive case that on a balance of probabilities it was in the interests of the child that the order should be made. This means that no factors in a case could be said to give rise to a presumption in favour of the order. However, there could be some factors which might often properly be regarded as important or even as carrying very great weight as long as they were assessed in the context of each case. The wish of the custodial parent to remove a child from the jurisdiction would always be a relevant factor, typically of very great weight.

HC *B v B (A Minor) (Residence Order)* [1992] 2 FLR 327

A child had lived with her grandmother since she was six weeks old. The mother still agreed that she should live there. The magistrates applying the no-order principle refused a residence order to the grandmother, on the basis that there was no risk of the child being removed from her care.

The application was by a carer with no parental authority, which was causing her problems with school and medical authorities. Since a residence order would confer the parental responsibility it followed that making the order must be better for the child than making no order at all.

6.4 The checklist

CA *Re W (A Minor) (Residence Order)* [1993] 2 FLR 625

A child was living with the maternal grandparents. A residence order was made in favour of the father, the court welfare recommendation being that the change of status quo would not cause such damage as would outweigh the right of the child to live with a parent.

It is the welfare of the child which is the test, but of course there is a strong supposition that, other things being equal, it is in the interests of the child that it shall remain with its natural parents, but that has to give way to particular needs in particular situations. On the facts, the judge was not plainly wrong, but fresh evidence required a rehearing.

6.5 Wishes and feelings

CA *Re M (Family Proceedings: Affidavits)* [1995] 2 FLR 100

The father applied for residence on the basis of the child's wishes expressed to him. She was 12 and living with her grandmother. The judge found both parents were able to care but that the child, despite her views, had no actual experience of living with the father. He followed the court welfare officer's 'instinct' that the child should live with the mother. The father appealed, producing affidavits sworn by himself and the child.

It was not the practice to allow children to intervene in family proceedings between their parents. Any attempt by a solicitor or counsel to boost a parent's case in the Court of Appeal by involving the child in swearing an affidavit was seriously deprecated. The judge quite clearly took the child's views into account. The weight to be given to those views was entirely a matter for him and was not appealable unless it was outside the ordinary commonsense approach of the experienced judge.

HC *Re S (Contact) (Children's Views)* [2002] 1 FLR 1156

A 16-year-old girl said she wanted only telephone calls with her father. A 14-year-old boy had not seen him for nine months, and wanted only pre-planned one-to-one contact. A 12-year-old son had been having contact with some difficulties. The father claimed the mother had caused the children to suffer 'parental alienation syndrome', and pursued contact to all three.

The judge made a declaration as to the ideal contact but no order as to the girl, and orders for contact by negotiation and agreement with the boys. The father did not listen to these young adolescents, who had understandably been upset by specific incidents. Children of this age were entitled to have their views respected. They should have been allowed to make decisions without the pressure of being asked to select between one parent and another. Compelling these children to have contact would be counter-productive. The alternative was preferable: to try persuasion, to give respect to their views, to acknowledge what they were saying, to listen to them and to provide opportunities for negotiation; in effect to treat them as young adults with minds of their own and opinions which were to be taken at face value without being criticised.

HHJ Tyrer

'If young people are to be brought up to respect the law, then it seems to me that the law must respect them and their wishes, even to the extent of allowing them, as occasionally they do, to make mistakes.'

6.6 Siblings

CA *C v C (Minors) (Custody)* [1988] 2 FLR 291

In a case just prior to the Children Act, a court gave custody of one child to each parent, with access to the other.

The siblings should not have been separated.

Purchas J

'It is really beyond argument that unless there are strong features indicating a contrary arrangement that brothers and sisters should, wherever possible, be brought up together, so that they are an emotional support to each other in the stormy waters of the destruction of their family.'

6.7 Equality of parents

CA *Re W (A Minor) (Residence Order)* [1992] 2 FLR 332

A judge made a residence order in favour of a father for a newborn baby. The mother said her prior agreement to that was under pressure and that she now wished to start breastfeeding. Her appeal was allowed.

There was no presumption of law that a child of any given age was better off with one parent or the other; the only legal principle involved was that the welfare of the child was the paramount consideration. However, there was a rebuttable presumption of fact that a baby's best interests were served by being with its mother, although the situation might be different with older children. Although there was a well-established principle that when inquiries were being made the *status quo* should not be disturbed, it was not really possible to establish a *status quo* within a period of three weeks at the beginning of the child's life.

6.8 Culture, religion and heritage

 Re P (Section 91(14) Guidelines) (Residence and Religious Heritage) **[1999] 2 FLR 573**

Because of family circumstances an Orthodox Jewish family were unable to care for a seriously disabled child. She was placed with non-practising Catholic foster-carers. The family made several attempts to have the child moved to Jewish foster-carers, but none could be found. The foster-carers obtained a residence order which the parents then sought to overturn.

In any decision about a child's upbringing the religious and cultural heritage of the child was a relevant consideration. When a religion which provided a way of life and permeated every activity formed part of the child's family background, the child's religious and cultural heritage was an important factor. It was not the court but family circumstances which had removed the child's ability to grow up in a Jewish household. The judge was entitled, on the evidence of the child's limited ability to understand and appreciate the Jewish religion, to conclude that her religious and cultural heritage was not an overwhelming factor in this case. The question of religion could only ever be one factor among many.

Re S (Specific Issue Order: Religion: Circumcision) [2005] I FLR 236

The children, one of whom was a boy approaching nine, were brought up by a Hindu father and Muslim mother, experiencing a mix of the religions. The mother separated from the father and wished to bring the children up solely as Muslims and to have the boy circumcised. Islam required circumcision, Hinduism forbade it.

The children of a mixed heritage should be allowed to decide for themselves which, if any, religion they wished to follow. Circumcision was not in the son's best interests at present, because it would limit his freedom of choice. The Muslim religion permitted circumcision later, at puberty, by which time the son would be *Gillick*-competent and could make an informed decision himself.

 Haringey London Borough Council v C (E, E, F and High Commissioner of Republic of Kenya Intervening) [2007] I FLR 1035

The child was brought to this country by a couple, Mr and Mrs E, who claimed he had been born to them as a 'miracle baby'. Their religious faith led them to believe that the conception and birth came about through the 'will of God', that placement of the child with others would not be permitted by God and that placement with themselves was divinely ordained. The court made an adoption order to foster carers.

Despite the respect given to private and family life, to freedom of thought, conscience and religion and any individual belief system, the law did not give religious belief or birthright a pre-eminent place in the balance of factors that comprised welfare. If the views of Mr and Mrs E were to be sanctioned, it would be virtually impossible for them to modify their position beyond their beliefs and the child would have to be encapsulated within that belief system and his future founded upon a lie. A placement with them would thus be contrary to the child's interests.

6.9 The *status quo*

HC **Diocco v Milne** (1983) 4 FLR 247

Each parent wished to care for their child. The magistrates found in favour of the father and the mother appealed.

There were three key factors important in child cases that the magistrates had failed to consider, namely:

(1) The desirability of continuity of care as an important part of a child's sense of security and the need to avoid the disruption of established bonds whenever possible.

(2) The desirability of avoiding, if possible, the division of the care of a child between several persons.

(3) The parent's attitude towards contact with the other parent.

6.10 Presumption for natural parents

CA *Re W (A Minor) (Residence Order)* [1993] 2 FLR 625

A child was living with the maternal grandparents. A residence order was made in favour of the child's father, the court welfare recommendation being that the change of *status quo* would not cause such damage as would outweigh the right of the child to live with a parent.

It is the welfare of the child which is the test, but of course there is a strong supposition that, other things being equal, it is in the interests of the child that it shall remain with its natural parents, but that has to give way to particular needs in particular situations. On the facts, the judge was not plainly wrong but fresh evidence required a rehearing.

CA *Re M (Child's Upbringing)* [1996] 2 FLR 441

In order to avoid a child having to go back to his village under apartheid regulations, an English woman living in South Africa took in the child of her Zulu maid as her own. She later returned from South Africa with the child and later applied to adopt the child. The parents sought wardship and immediate return of the child. The judge made a plan for the return of the child in two years' time. He was 10 and his wishes were to stay with the English carers.

In arriving at his decision the judge had referred to the competing claims of the appellant as the child's psychological parent and the mother as the child's biological parent. But the essential principle to be applied was that, other things being equal, it was in the interests of the child to be brought up by his natural parents. That was a guide to the competing claims in the present case. It was not determinative of the conclusion, for it must be subservient to the paramount consideration, which was the child's welfare. The child was returned to South Africa in five weeks.

In fact the child failed to settle and his subsequent return was agreed.

Re G (Children) [2006] UKHL 43

Two lesbian women brought children up together until separating. Following litigation, and contact arrangements being made, CG, the biological mother, secretly removed the children to Cornwall. Once they were traced she allowed contact with CW, the non-biological mother, and the matter came before the Court of Appeal who transferred residence to CW. The case then went to the House of Lords.

The Court of Appeal had not placed enough weight on the fact that CG was the biological mother, which whilst not raising a presumption, was an important factor in CG's favour. Both were regarded as psychological and social parents.

A child should not be removed from the care of biological parents without compelling reason. A change in primary residence was unlikely where contact with the other parent is being maintained.

6.11 Harm and the standard of proof

CA *Re M and R (Child Abuse: Evidence)* [1996] 2 FLR 195

Children made allegations of sexual abuse, excessive punishment and filthy living conditions. The judge found that although there was a real possibility that the sexual abuse had occurred, the evidence was not sufficient to prove the allegations to the requisite standard. He was able to find emotional abuse proved. The local authority appealed.

A court could not find that the children were at risk of sexual abuse in the future on the basis of a mere suspicion of sexual abuse in the past. Section 1(3)(e) dealt with actual harm or risk of harm and not with possibilities, and there was no justification for the proposition that because the welfare of the child was paramount, the standard of proof for establishing harm should be less than the preponderance of probabilities.

CHAPTER 7

PARENTAL RESPONSIBILITY

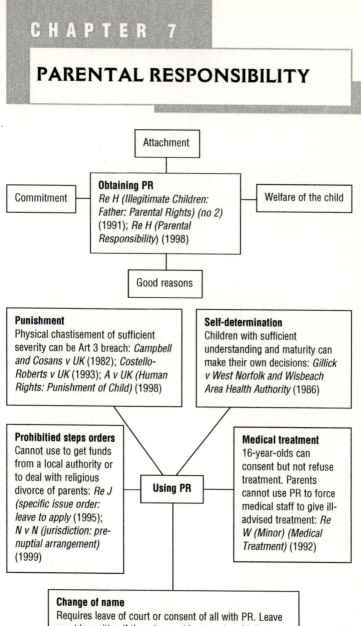

Attachment

Obtaining PR
Re H (Illegitimate Children: Father: Parental Rights) (no 2) (1991); *Re H (Parental Responsibility)* (1998)

Commitment

Welfare of the child

Good reasons

Punishment
Physical chastisement of sufficient severity can be Art 3 breach: *Campbell and Cosans v UK* (1982); *Costello-Roberts v UK* (1993); *A v UK (Human Rights: Punishment of Child)* (1998)

Self-determination
Children with sufficient understanding and maturity can make their own decisions: *Gillick v West Norfolk and Wisbeach Area Health Authority* (1986)

Prohibited steps orders
Cannot use to get funds from a local authority or to deal with religious divorce of parents: *Re J (specific issue order: leave to apply* (1995); *N v N (jurisdiction: pre-nuptial arrangement)* (1999)

Using PR

Medical treatment
16-year-olds can consent but not refuse treatment. Parents cannot use PR to force medical staff to give ill-advised treatment: *Re W (Minor) (Medical Treatment)* (1992)

Change of name
Requires leave of court or consent of all with PR. Leave must be written if there is a residence order: *Re T (Change of Surname)* (1998); *Dawson v Wearmouth* (1997); *Re PC (Change of surname)* (1997)

7.1 Obtaining parental responsibility

CA *Re H (Illegitimate Children: Father: Parental Rights)* (No 2) [1991] 1 FLR 214

Under legislation preceding the CA 1989 the father applied for parental rights. He acknowledged that he was not going to get custody of the children, and that he wanted these rights solely to participate in the adoption proceedings.

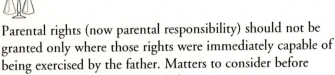

Parental rights (now parental responsibility) should not be granted only where those rights were immediately capable of being exercised by the father. Matters to consider before granting parental rights included:

(1) the level of commitment of the father
(2) the degree of attachment between father and child
(3) the reason of the father applying for the order.

CA *Re H (Parental Responsibility)* [1998] 1 FLR 855

A father who had inflicted serious injuries on his child was denied a parental responsibility order. He appealed, claiming that once he had fulfilled the three factors mentioned in *Re H (Illegitimate Children: Father: Parental Rights) (No 2)*, he was entitled to the order.

Those requirements were a starting point, not a exhaustive list. Although parental responsibility was a question of status, and different to applications under s 8 of the CA 1989, the child's welfare was still the paramount consideration. The judge was right on the facts not to make the order.

HC **D v Hereford and Worcester County Council** [1991] 2 FRL 205

A father in care proceedings obtained a parental rights order (the predecessor of parental responsibility) and the local authority objected, stating that it would confer rights of access and legal custody and was incompatible with the care order.

Parental rights gave only *locus standi* to apply to the courts for orders regulating his parental rights or to be heard in care proceedings. It does not prevent the local authority from exercising its parental rights over the child.

HC **Re M (Handicapped Child: Parental Responsibility)** [2001] 2 FLR 342

There had been much dispute over the care of a severely handicapped child, and the father's application for residence was refused and contact reduced.

The father had shown commitment and a high degree of attachment. His motivation for making the parental responsibility application was slightly suspect, but was to a significant extent concern for the child. However it would not be in the child's interests to grant the father a parental responsibility order in circumstances in which it was highly likely that he would misuse it to lend weight to future interference in her care, thereby continuing the stress on the mother and potentially undermining the mother's ability to care properly for the child.

HC *Re X (Parental Responsibility Agreement: Children in Care)*
[2000] 1 FLR 517

A local authority with a care order claimed they could determine the extent to which the mother could use her parental responsibility to prevent her granting the father parental responsibility.

The father does not exercise parental responsibility when signing a parental responsibility agreement, as he does not get parental responsibility until the agreement is lodged, so it could not be said that the grant by the mother was an exercise of parental responsibility. The LA could not stop the mother signing. Nor could the LA prevent a marriage which would automatically give parental responsibility.

7.2 Self-determination

HL *Gillick v West Norfolk and Wisbeach Area Health Authority* [1986] AC 112

Mrs Gillick objected to guidance given to doctors that, whilst it was unusual to give contraceptive or abortion advice to under-16-year-old children without parental consent, in some circumstances it would be lawful. When the authority refused to guarantee that no such advice would be given to her daughters without her consent, she sought a declaration that the guidance was unlawful and wrong and adversely affected her rights as a parent and that no advice could be given to her daughters.

(1) Parental rights are subject to the guiding principle that where the court had before it a question as to the care and upbringing of a child, it must treat the welfare of the child as paramount.

(2) Parental rights to control a child derived from parental duty and existed for the protection of the child. A parent's right to completely control a child diminishes as the child gains understanding. It ends completely when they are 18.

(3) Parental control yielded to the child's right to make his own decisions when he reached a sufficient understanding and intelligence to be capable of making up his own mind on the matter requiring decision. Parental authority was a dwindling right.

(4) The parental right to determine whether or not a child under 16 would have medical treatment ends if and when the child achieved a sufficient understanding and intelligence to enable him or her to understand fully what was proposed.

(5) In the overwhelming majority of cases, the best judges of a child's welfare were his parents, but exceptionally that was not the case.

(6) Since a child under 16 had the capacity to consent to medical treatment provided he or

she was capable of understanding what was proposed, and capable of expressing his or her own wishes, a girl under 16 of sufficient maturity and intelligence could give valid consent to contraceptive advice and treatment.

7.3 Parental responsibility and medical treatment

HC *Re C (A Child) (HIV Test)* [1999] 2 FLR 1004

An HIV-positive mother who was sceptical of medical treatments for AIDS and HIV breastfed her child. The local authority obtained a declaration that the child should be tested for HIV. The parents appealed.

The matter of testing the child was a question of the child's welfare, not the rights of the parents, and it was not in the best interests of the child for the health professionals to be unaware of the child's state of health. This decision did not however deal with more serious interventions in terms of the treatment given to the child if the test was positive for HIV.

CA *Re J (A minor) (Medical Treatment)* [1992] 2 FLR 165

A child suffered severe disabilities following a fall aged four weeks. Several experts opined that using a ventilator would be cruel. One disagreed. The mother sought a declaration that the hospital provide all interventional treatments including ventilation against their views.

A medical practitioner owed a fundamental duty to his patient, subject to obtaining any necessary consent, to treat the patient in accordance with his own best clinical judgment. Where a course of treatment was considered not to be in the best interests of the minor, it would be an abuse of judicial power in the exercise of its inherent jurisdiction to protect the interests of minors to require a medical practitioner or health authority acting by a medical practitioner directly or indirectly to treat the minor in a manner contrary to that fundamental duty and against his best clinical judgment.

CA *Re W (Minor) (Medical Treatment)* [1992] 4 All ER 627

A local authority cared for a 16-year-old anorexic self-harming girl. They sought a declaration under the inherent jurisdiction to give the girl medical treatment without her consent.

The common law allowed an under-16-year-old with sufficient understanding to consent to treatment. Section 8 Family Law Reform Act 1969 allowed a 16-year-old to consent. Neither gave an absolute right to refuse treatment. Anorexia affected the ability to give informed views and it was in the child's welfare to override the girl's refusal. The inherent jurisdiction also allowed the court to override consent by a child even where parents using their authority could not.

HC **Re L (Medical Treatment: Gillick Competency)** [1998] 2 FLR 810

A 14-year-old Jehovah's witness refused a blood transfusion which was necessary to save her life. She had sincere and mature beliefs, but was not aware of the exact nature of death she would suffer. The hospital sought a declaration as to whether she was competent to refuse treatment.

The child had lived a sheltered life, influenced by her congregation and without adult experience on which to base her decision. She had not been able to take in all the information. She was not competent and the treatment should be given.

HC **Re P (Medical Treatment Best Interests)** [2003] EWHC 2327 (Fam)

A 16-year-old Jehovah's witness boy refused a blood transfusion.

Leave was given to administer blood where no other treatment was available. In some cases where treatment prolonged death only for months, an older child's refusal could be determinative. Otherwise the court's duty is to ensure the child survives to reach the age of majority, when he is then free to exercise his autonomy.

7.4 Parental responsibility and punishment

Campbell and Cosans v United Kingdom (1982) 4 EHRR 293

Scottish schoolchildren complained that being punished with a belt was an Art 3 breach.

The degree of humiliation and degradation experienced by (potential) recipients of 'the belt' in schools was considered insufficient to invoke Art 3, the use of such punishment being at that time so traditional in Scottish schools that the applicants were neither humiliated nor debased in the eyes of others or of themselves to the requisite degree.

Costello-Roberts v UK (1993) 25 EHRR 112

A seven-year-old was subjected to corporal punishment at an English private school: three smacks, administered by a soft-soled shoe through the child's shorts, with no visible sign of injury.

Such treatment was considered insufficient to invoke Art 3.

A v United Kingdom (Human Rights: Punishment of Child)
[1998] 2 FLR 959

A stepfather admitted beating a nine-year-old child with a
garden cane. Bruising was caused. He claimed it was necessary
punishment and reasonable chastisement. A jury in a criminal
trial found him not guilty. The child claimed this breached his
Art 3 rights.

Beating with a garden cane applied with considerable force on
more than one occasion was ill-treatment of sufficient severity
to fall within Art 3. The state was required to take measures
designed to ensure that individuals, including children, were
not ill-treated in breach of Art 3 by other private individuals.
In permitting parents, and others *in loco parentis,* who had ill-
treated a child in breach of Art 3 to raise the defence of
'reasonable chastisement', the UK was failing to protect
children from such ill-treatment.

7.5 IVF treatment

HL *Re R (IVF: Paternity of a Child)* [2005] UKHL 33

A woman and a man commenced artificial insemination
treatment. The man signed a 'male partner's
acknowledgement', acknowledging that he intended to become
the legal father of any resulting child. Initial treatment was
unsuccessful and whilst waiting for *in vitro* treatment the man
signed a further acknowledgement. The first attempt failed

and the couple separated. The mother continued with treatment, failing to declare the separation but attending with a new partner. When the child was born the original partner obtained a declaration of paternity. The Court of Appeal allowed the mother's appeal against the declaration. The man appealed.

If the 'joint enterprise' of fertility treatment had ended by the time the successful treatment had begun, because by that stage the consenting couple had separated, the man was not the legal father of the resulting child. Legal certainty was important, but paternity should not be based on a fiction. A rule that until the man expressly withdrew his consent, he would be deemed the father, could produce some very undesirable and unjust consequences. His appeal was dismissed.

7.6 Prohibited steps orders

HC *Re J (Specific Issue Order: Leave to Apply)* [1995] 1 FLR 669

J, who was born in 1978, claimed to be a child 'in need' for the purposes of s 17 of the Children Act 1989. The local authority denied that J was in need. Leave was sought by J to make an application for a specific issue order deeming himself to be a child in need and requiring the local authority to make appropriate provision accordingly.

Judicial review is the only way to challenge the local authority's decision. A specific issue order would be inappropriate to determine the question of whether J was a child in need. Moreover, the question as to whether a child was in need was not one which arose in connection with any aspect of parental responsibility, which is a prerequisite for a specific issue order.

HC **N v N (Jurisdiction: Pre-Nuptial Arrangement)** [1999] 2 FLR 745

A Jewish couple entered into an ante-nuptial agreement which required them to comply with the ruling of the Beth Din in relation to matrimonial disputes. After separation they entered into a contact order which included a recital that the husband would progress the Jewish religious divorce expeditiously. He failed to do so and the wife tried to enforce the recital by way of a specific issue order.

As a matter of public policy the ante-nuptial agreement was not enforceable as a contract. There was no basis for an injunction, which meant that the recital could not be enforced by committal as an undertaking. It was not an exercise of parental responsibility so it could not be the subject of a specific issue order.

7.7 Changes of names

CA *Re T (Change of Surname)* [1998] 2 FLR 620

A mother had three children whose surname began with F. She then had twins with another man whose surname was T. After they split up she changed the names of the twins to F, the name she and the other children used. The father said that it should be T.

In any situation of dispute regarding children's names, either the consent of the other parent or the leave of the court was essential, certainly where both parents had parental responsibility. The twins should be called T, their father's name. Neither the convenience of using one name for medical and school records, nor the long period of unlawful use, justified the change of name.

CA *Dawson v Wearmouth* [1997] 2 FLR 629

The mother had two children by her husband. She had a child with another man and registered his child in her married surname. The father said that the child should take his name, even though he and the mother were no longer in a relationship.

(1) Section 13 CA 1989 prevents anyone causing a child to be known by a new surname without the leave of the court if there is a residence order.

(2) Where no residence order exists, whether or not the father had parental responsibility for the child, the court can make a specific issue order under s 8 deciding the name of the child.

(3) The registered name of the child was a major factor to be taken into account.

(4) Wearmouth had been the mother's actual name at the time it was chosen by her, as well as being the surname of the child's half-siblings. It was a logical choice for her to make and could not be criticised as alien simply because it was also the name of the mother's ex-husband. The child should use that name.

HC *Re PC (Change of Surname)* [1997] 2 FLR 1997

The children lived with their mother. She changed the children's surnames, but the school refused to comply with the deed poll she signed without reference to the father. There was no residence order and the mother contended that the Children Act 1989 allowed her to use her parental responsibility unilaterally.

By law, a parent did not have the right, power or authority unilaterally to change a legitimate child's surname without the consent of the other parent. Consent need not necessarily be given in writing, save where the child was the subject of a residence order or a care order. Where consent was not forthcoming, a court order was required. Where only one person had parental responsibility, he had the right and power lawfully to cause a change of surname.

That did not apply where a child had sufficient legal competence to change his own name or to consent to it, especially if the child was over 16.

Schools, doctors and other holders of 'official' or formal records should be satisfied that everyone with parental responsibility had consented to a change of surname or that there was a court order to that effect.

CA *Re W, Re A, Re B (Change of Name)* [1999] 2 FLR 930

All the appeals related to the circumstances in which one parent could have a child's name changed without the consent of the other.

(1) Registration was a relevant and important consideration, but not in itself decisive; the weight to be given to it by the court would depend upon the other relevant factors which might tip the balance the other way, including factors which might arise in the future.
(2) The fact that a child has a different name from the applicant would not generally carry much weight.
(3) The reasons for an earlier unilateral decision to change a child's name might be relevant, as might any changes of circumstance since the original registration. A marriage is important, and if the child had been registered under the father's surname, there would have to be strong reasons to change the child's name.

(4) Where the parents were unmarried, the degree of the father's commitment to the child, the quality of any contact and the existence or absence of parental responsibility were all relevant factors.

CA *Re R (Surname: Using both Parents')* [2001] 2 FLR 1358

The mother was going to Spain with her new husband and wished the child to use the step-father's surname.

The burden was on the parent seeking to obtain approval for a change of surname and it had to be shown that the change would be in the child's interests. In this case the couple were urged to consider the use of both parents' surnames, as was the tradition in Spain.

Hale LJ

'It is . . . a matter of great sadness to me that it is so often assumed, and even sometimes argued, that fathers need that outward and visible link in order to retain their relationship with, and commitment to, their child. That should not be the case. It is a poor sort of parent whose interest in and commitment to his child depends upon that child bearing his name. After all, that is a privilege which is not enjoyed by many mothers, even if they are not living with the child. They have to depend upon other more substantial things . . . In my judgment, parents and courts should be much more prepared to contemplate the use of both surnames in an appropriate case, because that is to recognise the importance of both parents.'

Re S (Change of Names: Cultural Factors) [2001] 2 FLR 1005

A Muslim mother and Sikh father eloped and had a son who had three recognisably Sikh names. Following divorce the mother applied to change the names to Muslim ones, which would allow her and the child to be accepted back into her community. She had previously used a Muslim nickname but because it was similar to the father's name, she wished to abandon that name.

The mother's reason to abandon the existing forename was flimsy, but Muslim names were needed for integration. The child would keep the existing name, add another Muslim name and be registered for health and education in those names. However, there was not to be a deed poll formally changing names, because retention of the Sikh names would represent the reality of his heritage. He could make a formal decision himself when older.

CHAPTER 8

PRIVATE CHILD LAW

RESIDENCE ORDERS: KEY POINTS

Shared residence orders

1. Do not require exceptional circumstance but must be in interest of the child: *D v D (Shared residence order)* (2001)
2. Can be between gay parents to confer PR; *G v F (Contact and Shared Residence: Applications for leave)* (1998)
3. Can be made even if there is a distance between the homes: *Re F (shared residence)* (2003)

Effect of residence orders

Gives the right to decide day-to-day issues affecting the child: *Re P (A Minor) (Parental Reponsibility Orders)* (1994)

Conditions on residence orders

Exceptionally can impose geographical constraints: *Re E (Residence: Imposition of Conditions)* (1997)

Leave applications

Parents without PR should usually be joined in: *Re P (Care Proceedings: Father's application to be joined in as a party)* (2001). The court should be aware of Art 8 rights

Section 91(14) directions

Not only for unreasonable and repeated applications but for child's welfare: *Re P (Section 91(14) Guidelines) (Residence and Religious Heritage)* (1999)

Only conditions are duration and type of application. Exceptionally can be until child is 16: *Re S (Children): Re E (A child)* (2006)

CONTACT ORDERS: KEY POINTS

Presumption in favour of contact

Child has right to know birth parents. Test is whether there are cogent reasons to deny that: *Re F (Contact; Restraint Order)* (1995); *Re H (Minors) (Access)* (1992)

Conditions

Wide discretion to impose conditions including positive ones to send information: *Re O (Contact: Imposition of Conditions)* (1995)

Enforcement

European law requires positive steps to ensure contact takes place: *Hansen v Turkey* (2004)

Implacably hostile parents may be imprisoned or residence changed: *A v N (Committal: Refusal of Contact)* (1997)

If lack of contact is causing significant harm on s 37 direction may be made.

Costs orders may be appropriate in enforcement processings: *Re F (Family Proceedings: Section 37 Investigation)* (2005)

Domestic violence

Proven violence may be cogent reason to refuse: *Re L (Contact: Domestic Violence); Re V (Contact: Domestic Violence); Re M (Contact: Domestic Violence); Re H (Contact: Domestic Violence)* (2000)

The court should consider the conduct of both parties towards each other and towards the children, the effect of the violence on the children and on the residential parent, and the motivation of the parent seeking contact.

8.1 Shared residence orders

CA *Re H (A Minor: Shared Residence Order)* [1994] 1 FLR 717

A father sought a shared residence order.

A shared residence order would only rarely be made and would depend upon exceptional circumstances. The child's welfare required that he should have a settled home, and giving him two competing homes would only lead to confusion and stress, and be contrary to the paramount concept of the welfare of the child himself. The order might be appropriate if it would reduce the differences between the parties.

CA *D v D (Shared Residence Order)* [2001] 1 FLR 495

The children spent substantial time with each parent, between whom there was animosity. The father sought shared residence, complaining that authorities treated him as a second class parent without it.

Contrary to earlier case law, it is not necessary to show that exceptional circumstances exist before a shared residence order may be granted. Nor is it probably necessary to show a positive benefit to the child. What is required is to demonstrate that the order is in the interest of the child in accordance with the requirements of s 1 of the Children Act 1989.

HC *G v F (Contact and Shared Residence: Applications for Leave)* [1998] 2 FLR 799

A lesbian co-parent of a child sought a shared residence order with the biological mother.

It is not inappropriate to use shared residence to give parental responsibility. The parties to a shared residence order do not have to be mother and father, and neither does there have to be equal periods in respect of the time spent in different households. There is no bias against lesbian co-parents.

CA *Re F (Shared Residence)* [2003] 2 FLR 397

Mother was given leave to live with the children in Scotland. The very committed father had generous contact in England, but appealed a shared residence order, seeking sole residence.

A shared residence order can be made even where there is a considerable distance between the parent's homes. It must reflect the underlying reality of where the children lived their lives, and was not made to deal with issues of parental status, but it is not the case that it requires even alternation between the homes. If the home offered by each parent was of equal status and importance to the children an order for shared residence could be valuable.

8.2 Effect of a residence order

 Re P (A Minor) (Parental Responsibility Orders) [1994] 1 FLR 578

Bad feeling existed between two parents. The magistrates granted the father a contact order, but dismissed his application for a parental responsibility order on the basis that because of the acrimony between the parents, the father could use the order to question aspects of the child's upbringing unnecessarily.

An order for parental responsibility to the father did not give him a right to interfere in matters within the day-to-day management of the child's life or to override the decision of the mother. The mother's residence order gave her the right to decide day-to-day issues affecting the child, and a parental responsibility order would not authorise the father to interfere in those decisions.

8.3 Conditions on residence orders

CA *Re E (Residence: Imposition of Conditions)* [1997] 2 FLR 638

A judge made residence orders in respect of the children in favour of the mother but imposed a requirement under s 11(7) of the Children Act 1989 that the children continue to reside at a named address unless otherwise ordered or agreed to by the father. The mother appealed.

Section 11(7) of the 1989 Act is wide enough to enable courts to make orders with restrictions on residence to specified places within the UK. However, a general imposition of requirements (subject to exceptional cases) on residence orders was not intended by Parliament and where a parent was, as here, an entirely suitable carer, a condition of residence at a set address was an unwarranted imposition on the right of the parent to choose where she would live within the UK and with whom.

HC *B v B (Residence: Condition Limiting Geographic Area)*
[2004] 2 FLR 979

The mother had made two previous applications to remove the child to Australia. She now wished to move from the South of England to the North. It was clear that the mother was intransigently opposed to contact between child and father. Mindful of cases such as *Re E (Residence: Imposition of Conditions)* [1997] 2 FLR 638, the father applied for a specific issue order to require the mother to educate the child at school in the South, and wardship.

The judge made a residence order in the mother's favour, with a condition that she and the child should reside within an area bounded by the A4 to the north, the M25 to the west and the A3 to the south and east until further order. The real question was whether the proposed move was in the child's best interests. Wardship was not needed because s 11(7) CA 1989 allowed conditions on a residence order in exceptional circumstances such as this where the mother's motive was to get away from the father.

8.4 Presumption in favour of contact

CA *Re F (Contact; Restraint Order)* [1995] 1 FLR 956

The mother was implacably hostile to contact. An order was made for the children to be assessed by a child psychiatrist and an order made under s 91(14) CA 1989 against the father. The assessment did not happen but the father was refused permission to make further application. He appealed.

The s 91(14) order was to provide a quiet period during the assessment, not because the father was a vexatious litigant. Its purpose had failed. Leave should be given. The courts were determined to preserve the right of a child to know his non-custodial parent, and a custodial parent would not, save in the most exceptional circumstances, be permitted to deprive a child of that right through his or her own obduracy.

CA *Re H (Minors) (Access)* [1992] 1 FLR 148

A contact application by a father was refused. Three years later another application was refused, on the grounds that renewal of contact might upset the children and be of no benefit. The father appealed.

No court should deprive a child of access to either parent unless it was wholly satisfied that it was in the interests of the child that access should cease, and that was a conclusion at which the court should be extremely slow to arrive. Short-term upset of reintroducing contact should be weighed against the long-term advantage to the child of keeping in touch with the parent concerned. Save in exceptional cases, to deprive a parent of access was to deprive a child of an important contribution to his emotional and material growing-up in the long-term. The test to be applied was whether there were any cogent reasons why the children should be denied the opportunity of access to their natural father.

8.5 Conditions on contact orders

CA *Re O (Contact: Imposition of Conditions)* [1995] 2 FLR 124

The mother appealed a condition placed on a contact order, as she did not want to come into contact with the father herself. She was also opposed to the child having contact.

Section 11(7) of the Children Act 1989 conferred wide and comprehensive powers on the court to ensure contact between the child and the non-custodial parent, where it promoted the welfare of the child. The powers include ordering a parent to send information about a child to the other parent. The parents' interests were only relevant where they affected the welfare of the child. Where parents were separated, it was almost always in the child's interests to have contact with the other parent.

8.6 Enforcement of contact orders

HC *Thomason v Thomason* [1985] FLR 214

Bush J

'Questions of punishment for past behaviour or concepts of
the damage to the dignity of the court if an order is disobeyed
should not enter into consideration in a domestic jurisdiction
of this kind. The object of the exercise is to enforce the
breached order for access in the sense of getting it working, or
putting something more workable in its place. This is rarely
achieved by sending a parent to prison or by fining them.
Indeed, the odds are that such an approach will only serve to
aggravate the hostility that already may exist between the
parties.'

CA *Re F (Contact: Restraint Order)* [1995] 1 FLR 956

Waite LJ

'The starting-point, always, is that every child has a right to be
brought up in knowledge of his non-custodial parent. That is
a right which the courts are determined to preserve, and they
will not – save in the most exceptional circumstances – allow a
custodial parent to deprive the child of the benefit of it
through his or her own obduracy – or (I would add) by
adopting an attitude which results in the child itself becoming
averse to contact with the non-custodial parent.'

ECHR *Hansen v Turkey* [2004] 1 FLR 142

Icelandic courts gave the mother custody of the children. The father took them to Turkey. Over 10 years of protracted proceedings, both civil and criminal, the mother saw the children on only three occasions. The mother complained to the European Court of Human Rights that the Turkish authorities had failed to enforce effectively her right of access to her children, in accordance with their positive obligation to respect family life under Art 8 of the European Convention on the Protection of Human Rights and Fundamental Freedoms 1950.

The Turkish authorities should have taken measures to allow the mother access to the children, including realistic coercive measures against the father of a type which were likely to lead to compliance. The Turkish authorities had failed to make adequate and effective efforts to enforce the mother's rights of access to the children. They had failed to seek the advice of social services or the assistance of psychologists or child psychiatrists in order to facilitate the mother's reunion with the children and to create a more co-operative atmosphere between the parents. This was a breach of Art 8.

ECHR *Zwadaka v Poland* [2005] 2 FLR 897

A father complained that the authorities had not done what they should to secure contact between him and his son.

The obligation of the national authorities to take measures to facilitate contact by a non-custodial parent was not absolute. The question was whether the authorities had taken all necessary steps to facilitate contact as could reasonably be demanded in the circumstances of each case. A lack of co-operation between parents was not a circumstance which could alone exempt the authorities from their positive obligations under Art 8. The authorities were obliged to take measures which would reconcile the conflicting interests of the parties. They failed to do so in this case, thus breaching Art 8.

CA *M v M (Breaches of Orders: Committal)* [2005] EWCA Civ 1722

There was an order that there should be no direct contact between the father and the children, prohibiting the father from allowing the children to enter his home and to remain with him, and directing him to return them immediately to their mother should they approach him. The father used to meet the children in town and breached the order on over 60 occasions. The mother sought his committal. It was refused and she appealed.

The judge was right to consider the impact of any committal on the welfare of the children. In this case the consequence was that the children might well become beyond parental control and need to be taken into care. The court was not plainly wrong in refusing to commit.

CA *A v N (Committal: Refusal of Contact)* [1997] 1 FLR 533

A mother flouted numerous contact orders. A suspended committal order was made, with a further contact order which she again breached. She was sentenced to prison. She appealed.

When considering whether to commit a mother to prison for flagrant breach of court orders requiring a child to have contact with the father, the welfare of the child was a material consideration but not the paramount consideration. There was a limit to the tolerance of the court when faced with persistent intransigence to its orders. The judge in the present case had been mindful of the effect of separation of mother and child and had exercised his discretion properly when he committed the mother to prison.

HC *Re F (Family Proceedings: Section 37 Investigation)* [2005] EWHC 2935 (Fam)

The children (who were separately represented by the National Youth Advocacy Service) lived with the father. He was opposed to all contact with the mother. NYAS, supported by the mother, sought a direction under s 37 CA 1989.

The threshold of emotional harm was satisfied by the father's attitude towards the mother, his refusal to let the children be seen, his complete subjugation of their views and their reaction and attitude to their mother (in which he was complicit). It was likely that extensive therapy would be required to correct the damage caused by their antipathy to their mother. However, there had to be no alternative before a s 37 order was made which could result in the boys being removed for assessment or separated from their father. A s 37 order could be avoided if the father consented to the boys seeing a child psychiatrist. If he did not comply, s 37 would then be appropriate.

CA *Re T (Order for Costs)* [2005] EWCA Civ 311, [2005] 2 FLR 681

In protracted Children Act proceedings the father, who ultimately was awarded a residence order, was awarded costs of several hearings. The mother claimed that although she had been irrationally anxious about contact, that was a function of her personality and she had not been wilfully unreasonable.

There was a limit to any allowance which could be made for a parent who deliberately and unreasonably obstructed contact in circumstances where, on an objective analysis, contact was in the interests of the child. The mother could not rely on her own irrational anxieties to bring her conduct within the band of reasonable behaviour. Once findings of fact had been made and a declaration made that contact was in the interest of the child, a parent who did not implement the order was acting unreasonably, which could lead to a costs order against them.

HC *Re D (Intractable Contact Dispute: Publicity)* [2004] EWHC 727 (Fam)

The mother was intractably opposed to contact. She had 'sabotaged contact arrangements by means of threadbare excuses and groundless assertions and allegations' over a period of five years, resulting in court orders, penal notices, suspended prison sentences and finally a period of imprisonment. There were 43 hearings conducted by 16 different judges after numerous adjournments. The parents' and experts' evidence totalled 950 pages.

The court system as it existed had failed to get to grips with the problem and to enforce contact.

Munby J

'Some – it may, for all I know, be many – of the fathers who are so critical of the system have only themselves to blame for the predicament in which they and their children find themselves and seek unfairly and inappropriately to turn their feelings of frustration and anger into criticism of the system. But the anger which some fathers display to the system cannot simply be put down to "the rage of Caliban seeing his own face in the glass". Some – in the nature of things I cannot know how many but I fear it is too many for comfort – have every justification for their feelings.

…

We can no longer simply complacently assume that our conventional domestic approach to such cases meets the standards required by Art 6 and Art 8.'

Some of his concerns about the current system were:

- The sheer length of proceedings: five years
- The large number of hearings and the astonishing number of judges
- 'A ceaseless proliferation of paper [which] is in large measure the product of delay; every time the case is adjourned further reports and statements are needed'

- The adjournment of final hearings which were prejudicial to the father's case
- The great delay in making findings
- The delay in seeking assistance from any expert other than the Court Welfare Officer
- The even longer delay before appointment of a children's guardian
- The characteristic judicial response when difficulties with contact emerged, which is absolutely central to the father's complaints; reduce the amount of contact and replace unsupervised with supervised
- The lack of overall timetable and the failure of the court to stick to such timetable as has been set
- The court's failure to get to grips with the mother's defiance of its own order and the court's failure to enforce its orders.

8.7 Children and domestic violence

CA *Re L (Contact: Domestic Violence); Re V (Contact: Domestic Violence); Re M (Contact: Domestic Violence); Re H (Contact: Domestic Violence)* [2000] 2 FLR 334

In all four cases there had been findings of domestic violence by the father against the mother, and contact had been refused. The fathers all appealed. The court sought guidance from child psychologists as to the effect of domestic violence on children.

Guidance was given for the conduct of cases involving allegations of domestic violence:

(1) The court should consider the conduct of both parties towards each other and towards the children, the effect of the violence on the

children and on the residential parent, and the motivation of the parent seeking contact.

(2) At an interim hearing, before findings, the court should give particular consideration to the likely risk of harm to the child, whether physical or emotional, if contact were granted or refused.

(3) The court should ensure, as far as possible, that any risk of harm to the child was minimised and that the safety of the child and the residential parent was secured before, during and after any such contact.

(4) Where allegations of domestic violence were made which might have an effect on the outcome, those allegations must be adjudicated upon, and found proved or not proved.

(5) There was no presumption that on proof of domestic violence the offending parent had to surmount a *prima facie* barrier of no contact, but violence was a factor in the balancing exercise of discretion carried out by the judge applying the welfare principle and the welfare checklist in s 1(1) and (3) of the Children Act 1989.

(6) In cases of proved domestic violence, the court had to weigh the seriousness of the domestic violence, the risks involved and the impact on the child against the positive factors, if any, of contact.

(7) The ability of the offending parent to recognise his past conduct, to be aware of the need to change and to make genuine efforts to do so would be likely to be an important consideration when performing that balancing exercise.

HC *Re A (Contact: Witness Protection Scheme)* [2005] EWCH 2189 Fam

There were findings that the child was at risk of being harmed through abduction to Pakistan or by virtue of the mother being subjected to violence by the father and his extended family. The uncle had been imprisoned for violence to the mother, which temporarily reduced the risk. The police had placed the mother in a witness protection programme. The child's guardian questioned whether the risk was high enough to justify that and said that the child needed direct contact. The court found that the measures taken in the face of fluctuating risk were justified.

Arrangements for contact could not be allowed to threaten the secret address of the mother and child so face-to-face contact was impossible. However, contact by video link with time delay should be tried, with a review of the risk in one year's time.

8.8 Applications for leave

CA *Re J (Leave to Issue Application for Residence Order)* [2003] 1 FLR 114

The mother could not care for a child, due to mental illness. The local authority assessed the maternal grandmother, but concluded that at the age of 59, bringing up the child would simply be too great a burden. They favoured adoption and objected to the grandmother's application for leave to apply for residence, on the basis that it was understandable but unrealistic.

The test is not 'has the applicant satisfied the court that he or she has a good arguable case'. The court must look at the s 10(9) CA 1989 checklist. The minimum essential protection of a grandparent's Arts 6 and 8 rights when making such an application was that judges were careful not to dismiss their applications without full inquiry.

HC *Re P (Care Proceedings: Father's Application to be Joined in as a Party)* **[2001] 1 FLR 781**

The natural father, who did not have parental responsibility, was at early hearings in this care case and was repeatedly advised to seek legal advice. He only applied to be a party at the final directions hearing some 18 months later. It was refused, on the basis that to join him would cause delay contrary to the child's welfare. He appealed.

As a general rule and unless there was some justifiable reason for not joining him, a natural father should be permitted to participate as a party in care proceedings relating to his child. However, here there was no breach of the father's human rights in refusing to allow him to be joined as a party to the proceedings. He had been given ample opportunity to be joined but had declined to take action. The denial of the father's right of access to the court was justified by the legitimate aim of resolving the care issue without further delay, and was proportionate to that aim.

8.9 Section 91(14) orders

CA *Re P (Section 91(14) Guidelines) (Residence and Religious Heritage)* [1999] 2 FLR 573

Guidance was given on s 91(14) orders:

(1) The leave restriction should generally be seen as a useful weapon of last resort in cases of repeated and unreasonable applications; in cases where the welfare of the child required it, a court could impose the restriction for other reasons.

(2) In such cases the court would need to be satisfied that the facts went beyond the commonly encountered need for time to settle to a new regime and the common situation in which there was animosity between the adults concerned.

(3) There would have to be a serious risk that without the imposition of the restriction, the child or primary carers would be subject to unacceptable strain.

(4) A s 91(14) restriction was not in breach of the European Convention on the Protection of Human Rights and Fundamental Freedoms 1950, as it did not deny access to the court, only access to an immediate hearing.

CA *Re S (Children): Re E (A Child)* [2006] EWCA Civ 1190

In both cases, long-term s 91(14) orders were made and the father required to get further information to justify the leave application before it was made.

It was not permissible to attach conditions to a s 91(14) order, beyond stating its duration and identifying the type of relief to which it applied.

A s 91(14) order could properly be made without limit of time, or for the period over which the court had jurisdiction to make orders in relation to children under s 8 of the Act, *Re P* applied. That was normally up to the age of 16. An order that was indeterminate, or which was expressed to last until a child was 16, was in effect an acknowledgement by the court that nothing more could be done. If the court had reached that stage, it had to spell out its reasons clearly.

8.10 Separate representation of children

HC *Re H (A Minor) (Role of Official Solicitor)* [1993] 2 FLR 552

A troubled child was represented by the official solicitor but applied to remove him as his guardian. He wished to defend the wardship application by instructing a solicitor directly.

The court must be satisfied that the child has 'sufficient understanding' to participate as a party in the proceedings without a guardian *ad litem*. That was more than instructing a solicitor as to his own views, and included giving evidence and being cross-examined, hearing the evidence and cross-examination of other parties and giving instructions and making decisions as matters arise. The sufficient understanding test must be considered in the light of all the circumstances of the case and in the light of what has already happened as well as what is likely to happen in the course of the proceedings in the future. When applying the test the court should not take into account what may or may not be in the best interests of the child.

8.11 Removal of a child from the jurisdiction

CA *Payne v Payne* [2001] 1 FLR 1052

A mother sought to remove a child to New Zealand.

Domestic case law on removal from the jurisdiction did not conflict with the Convention on the Protection of Human Rights and Fundamental Freedoms 1950.

There was no presumption in favour of the resident parent just because of the proposition that refusal was likely to damage the child's welfare. The reasonable proposals of the resident parent carried great weight, but had to be carefully scrutinised. Motivation for the move must be genuine, and not to end contact with the other parent. The courts should look at the effect of the refusal of leave and the effect of granting it on contact.

CHAPTER 9

CHILDREN IN NEED

Section 17 CA 1989 requires a child's needs to be assessed separately to those of the whole family: *R v Tower Hamlets London Borough Council ex p Bradford* (1998)

CHILDREN IN NEED

Social Services can use their powers under s 17 to provide accommodation. However, they are entitled to reserve that help to extreme cases and not provide a safety net to all families: *R (on the application of W) v Lambeth London Borough Council* (2002)

The duty owed by local authorities to children in need under s 17 of the Children Act 1989 is a target duty owed to children in general and is not justiciable by judicial review: *A v London Borough of Lambeth* (2001)

9.1 Assessing need

R v Tower Hamlets London Borough Council ex p Bradford
[1998] 1 FCR 629

A disabled mother and child with special educational needs were being harassed in the local authority flat in which they lived. They applied for rehousing and were given no points and placed at the bottom of the list. They appealed, claiming *inter alia* that the authority had failed to assess the child as a child in need under s 17 CA 1989.

For the purposes of s 17 of the 1989 Act, a local authority did not fulfil their statutory duty in respect of a child in need by considering his needs for rehousing along with the needs of the entire family, since different considerations might well apply. Whilst it might be reasonable for the family as a whole to stay where they were for some time, particularly if the parents were taking an unreasonably restrictive view of the area to which they were to move to, it was necessary for the authority to also consider what effect a prolonged stay in the accommodation would have on the child's development even if it resulted from the unreasonable attitude of the parents. Those were all matters that required assessment. On the facts, there was no evidence that such an assessment had been made.

R (On the application of W) v Lambeth London Borough Council [2002] EWCA Civ 613

A mother was homeless because of rent arrears. The Housing Authority would not provide accommodation, saying the arrears made her intentionally homelesss. The local authority assessed the needs of the children under s 17 CA 1989 but denied help with housing because there was nothing extreme in the facts of the case. The mother sought judicial review of the decision.

Social Services could use their powers under s 17 to provide accommodation. However, it was entitled to reserve that help to extreme cases and not provide a safety net to all families.

9.2 Generality of duties

A v London Borough of Lambeth [2001] EWHC 376 (Admin)

Disabled children were in unsuitable accommodation. It was accepted that they were 'children in need'. The mother sought judicial review of the failure to rehouse the family, arguing that the authority had a specific, enforceable duty to rehouse them under s 17. The local authority argued that its duty under s 17 was a general duty to pursue broad objectives, and was owed to local children collectively rather than to individuals.

The duty owed by local authorities to children in need under s 17 Children Act 1989 was a target duty owed to children in general and was not justiciable by judicial review. It was different to the s 20 duty to provide accommodation for children in specified circumstances. Even if the children had been assessed as needing accommodation, there was no enforceable duty under s 17 to provide that accommodation.

CHAPTER 10

EMERGENCY CHILD PROTECTION

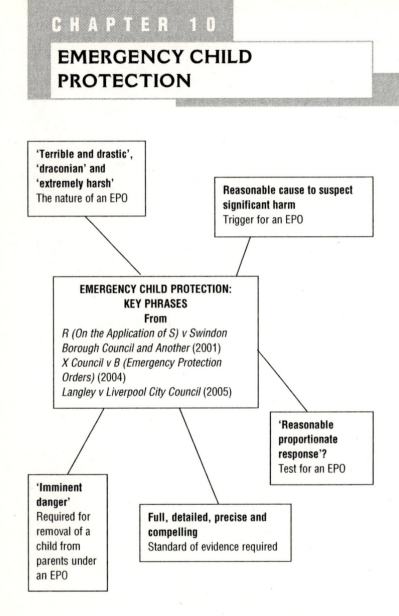

'Terrible and drastic', 'draconian' and 'extremely harsh'
The nature of an EPO

Reasonable cause to suspect significant harm
Trigger for an EPO

EMERGENCY CHILD PROTECTION:
KEY PHRASES
From
R (On the Application of S) v Swindon Borough Council and Another (2001)
X Council v B (Emergency Protection Orders) (2004)
Langley v Liverpool City Council (2005)

'Reasonable proportionate response'?
Test for an EPO

'Imminent danger'
Required for removal of a child from parents under an EPO

Full, detailed, precise and compelling
Standard of evidence required

10.1 The test for an Emergency Protection Order

QBD *R (On the Application of S) v Swindon Borough Council and Another* [2001] 3 FCR 702

The claimant was acquitted of abusing a child, K. He wished to begin living with a woman who also had a child. The father objected to the claimant's presence near his child. The local authority ultimately wrote the claimant a letter stating that there was a need to protect other children from the claimant. They took the view that on a balance of probabilities, K's allegations were true. They took the view that the claimant was likely to present a medium to high risk of some form of sexual abuse to children who were not related to him and that the most risk would be in relation to children who lived in the same house. The claimant applied for judicial review, submitting that the defendants had to be satisfied of the likelihood of significant harm.

A local authority's duty under s 47 CA 1989 was triggered by reasonable cause to suspect, not reasonable cause to believe that a child was likely to suffer significant harm. The need to establish facts on the balance of probability had no place in the exercise by a local authority of its various protective responsibilities. Accordingly, the threshold was quite low. The fact of an acquittal in criminal sexual abuse cases did not mean that a local authority was thereby absolved from further responsibility to protect the child who had made the allegations or any other children who might be in some way at risk.

10.2 Limits on the use of EPOs

HC   *X Council v B (Emergency Protection Orders)*
[2004] EWHC 2015 (Fam)

(1) EPOs are 'terrible and drastic', 'draconian' and 'extremely harsh'. An EPO should not be made unless the magistrates had been satisfied that it was both necessary and proportionate and that no other less radical form of order would promote the welfare of the child.

(2) There are features of them which may well not be compatible with European Human Rights standards (e.g. It need only be served 48 hours after it is made, there is no appeal against making or extending an EPO, no application for discharge can be made until 72 hours have elapsed, there is no appeal against the refusal to discharge an EPO, etc).

(3) EPOs should not automatically be made for the full eight days possible. Only in wholly exceptional cases should an order be made without notice to the parents, and then the parents are entitled to a full record of what happened.

(4) 'Imminent danger' must be proved before a child should be removed from parents under an EPO.

(5) The authority have a duty to keep EPOs under review and to allow reasonable contact.

 Munby J

'[Local Authorities should] approach every application for an EPO with an anxious awareness of the extreme gravity of the relief being sought

> and a scrupulous regard for the European
> Convention rights of both the child and the
> parents. . . .
>
> [I]t has even been suggested, though I express no
> views on the matter, that removal without having
> first considered alternative ways of safeguarding the
> child and therefore in breach of s 44(5), would not
> only merely be *ultra vires* but also expose the local
> authority to an action on behalf of the child for
> false imprisonment.'

CA *Langley v Liverpool City Council* **[2005] EWCA Civ 1173**

The father, who was registered blind and deaf, continued to
drive the children by car. The authority obtained an EPO but,
after it was granted, it was in fact the police who removed one
of the children from the home, using police protection powers
under s 46 CA 1989. The parents and child said that their
Art 8 rights had been breached.

Section 46 powers can be used when there is an EPO.
However, if the police know of the EPO, they should only use
s 46 if there is a compelling reason to do so and only when it
was not practical to use the EPO. Here the police should have
called an out-of-hours social worker to remove the child using
the EPO. The use of s 46 was a breach of human rights. In
the circumstances the obtaining of an EPO was a reasonable
and proportionate response to the situation, since a blind man
driving is a danger to himself and everyone affected by his
driving.

HC *Re X (Emergency Protection Orders)* [2006] EWHC 510 (Fam)

An EPO was obtained on the basis of fears of emotional abuse, including concerns about fabricated illness by the mother, although there was no medical evidence for this. Concerns were raised about sexual abuse which were later abandoned. A number of misleading, incomplete, or wrong statements were made in the course of the local authority's evidence.

Imminent danger must be actually established for an EPO. The evidence must be full, detailed, precise and compelling. An EPO will rarely be warranted in cases of emotional abuse, cases of sexual abuse where the allegations are inchoate and non-specific, and where there is no evidence of the immediate risk of harm to the child, or cases of fabricated or induced illness where there is no medical evidence of immediate risk of direct physical harm to the child.

CHAPTER 11

CARE AND SUPERVISION ORDERS

STARTING CARE PROCEEDINGS

Which local authority?

Care order goes to authority where children ordinarily resident.
Habitual or ordinary residence could be lost in a single day but could not be gained elsewhere save following an appreciable period of time: *Re C (Care order: Appropriate Local Authority)* (1997)

The threshold criteria

- Must be satisfied at time of intervention: *Southwark London Borough Council v B* (1998)
- Could be satisfied when there was no more than a possibility that parents, rather than one of the other carers, were responsible for inflicting the injuries which the child had suffered: *Lancashire County Council v B* (2000)
- The court will use the objective standard of the hypothetical reasonable person but cannot simply ignore the underlying cultural, social or religious realities: *A Local Authority v N and Others* (2005)
- Passing threshold does not automatically mean a care order
- Significant harm must be something unusual, more than commonplace human failure or inadequacy: *Re L (Care Threshold Criteria)* (2007)

Unidentified abusers

If the child has been harmed in the care of two parents who cannot be distinguished, both should be treated as perpetrators: *Re CB and JB (minors) (Care proceedings: case conduct)* (1998)

Standard of proof

Ordinary civil standard of the balance of probabilities remembering that the more improbable the event the stronger must be the evidence that it did occur: *Re H and others (Minors) (Sexual Abuse: Standard of Proof)* (1996)

Notice to potential parties

- A father without PR ought to be joined in unless there was some justifiable reason for not joining him as a party: *Re B (Care Proceedings: Notification of Father without Parental Responsibility)* (1999)
- There is a discretion not to notify him if that is in the interest of the child: *Re X (Care: Notice of Proceedings)* (1996)

11.1 Definition of normal residence

HC *Re C (Care order: Appropriate Local Authority)* [1997] I FLR 544

Children who were subject to an interim care order but remained at home with their mother moved from one local authority area to another. The question was which one should have the care orders.

The mother was providing the accommodation, not the local authority, so s 105(6)(c) CA 1989 did not apply. The care order went to the local authority in which the child was ordinarily resident. Habitual or ordinary residence could be lost in a single day, but could not be gained elsewhere save following an appreciable period of time. The children, by moving from one area to another, ceased to be ordinarily resident in the first area but they had not been residing long enough in the second area to have acquired ordinary residence there. Therefore, the designated authority was the first one because that was the authority 'within whose area the circumstances arose etc.'.

Gateshead Metropolitan Borough Council v L and another
[1996] 2 FLR 179

A child was born and sometimes accommodated in Brent. In 1987 he moved to Gateshead and that authority obtained a care order. In 1992 he was accommodated by Gateshead until 1995, when he was placed under an interim care order and secure accommodation order. In 1994 the mother returned to Brent but the child was there for one night only. Each local authority said the other should be designated as the local authority holding the final care order

The first question to be asked was whether the child was ordinarily resident in the area of an authority. His placements since 1992 had to be disregarded by virtue of s 105(6) CA 1989. In this case the child's ordinary residence was not in the area of any authority for the purposes of s 31(8)(a) CA 1989. Section 31(8)(b) applied only 'where the child does not reside in the area of a local authority'. Parliament had accidentally omitted the word 'ordinarily' between 'not' and 'reside', and the Act should be read as if the word was there. Where s 31(8)(b) arose, more than one local authority could qualify for designation and in that event the court could choose which area to designate. Brent should be designated, as they had accepted paying the costs of keeping the child in secure accommodation and the family lived in Brent's area.

11.2 Time for satisfying the threshold criteria

Southwark London Borough Council v B [1998] 1 FLR 1095

The local authority sought care orders in respect of two children. The mother submitted that when the court was considering whether it had jurisdiction to make a care order or a supervision order, the relevant date for assessing whether the children were likely to suffer significant harm, under the second limb of s 31(2)(a) of the Children Act 1989, was the date of the hearing.

The relevant date in respect of both actual harm and the likelihood of harm was the date upon which the local authority initiated protective arrangements for the relevant child, so long as such protective arrangements had been continuously in place from the time of such intervention and initiation until disposal of the case by the court. Under the two-stage process, whereby the court had first to satisfy itself that the threshold criteria had been met and then go on to satisfy itself that the making of the care order was better for the child than making no order, the court was able to consider any subsequent developments at the second stage.

11.3 The objective nature of the test

Lancashire County Council v B [2000] 1 FLR 1095

A child suffered head injuries after a shaking incident. The judge could not tell whether it was caused by the parents or the babysitter. The babysitter's child was unharmed. The Court of Appeal said that a care order for the injured child should be made anyway, as the child had clearly suffered significant harm. The parents appealed on the grounds that, for the care order to be made, the harm had to be attributable to the parents, and citing Art 8.

The threshold conditions could be satisfied when there was no more than a possibility that the parents, rather than one of the other carers, were responsible for inflicting the injuries which the child had suffered. The court had to be satisfied that harm suffered by the child was attributable to 'the care given to the child'. That phrase referred primarily to the care given by a parent or parents or other primary carers, but could include the care given by any of the carers. The court had to be able to protect a child even when the perpetrator was not known. The fact that the threshold was passed did not automatically mean a care order would be made. There was no Art 8 breach because the steps taken were those reasonably necessary to pursue the legitimate aim of protecting the child from further injury.

No care order was made on the babysitter's child as he had not suffered significant harm and the threshold could not be crossed.

HC *A Local Authority v N and Others* [2005] EWHC 2956 (Fam)

A local authority were concerned about a Kurdish girl, who had gone through a ceremony of marriage at 15. She was placed with carers but returned home and was divorced in a further ceremony. She feared being sent to Iraq and being made to marry one of her cousins. However she returned home. The local authority sought a supervision order and orders under the inherent jurisdiction preventing her from leaving the jurisdiction until she reached the age of 18 and from marrying without the consent of the court.

The court when using the objective standard of the hypothetical reasonable person cannot simply ignore the underlying cultural, social or religious realities. The court must always be sensitive to the cultural, social and religious circumstances of the particular child and family. It should be slow to find that parents only recently arrived from a foreign country have fallen short of an acceptable standard of parenting if in truth they have done nothing wrong by the standards of their own community.

These days the only justification for wardship is if the child needs to be protected. The court would not interfere with the aspect of parental responsibility involved in giving consent to marriage unless the parents would not protect the child or she needed protection from the parents themselves. The test for interference in a case like this is whether there is a real possibility of harm.

HC *Re L (Care: Threshold Criteria)* [2007] Fam Law 297

Making findings of domestic violence, identifying the children as children in need, and acknowledging that the children had suffered harm in the past and were likely to do so in the future, attributable to the parenting they received, the judge noted that significant harm must be something unusual, more than commonplace human failure or inadequacy.

Hedley J

'Society must be willing to tolerate very diverse standards of parenting, including the eccentric, the barely adequate and the inconsistent. Children will inevitably have both very different experiences of parenting and very unequal consequences flowing from it. It means that some children will experience disadvantage and harm, while others flourish in atmospheres of loving security and emotional stability. These are the consequences of our fallible humanity and it is not the province of the state to spare children all the consequences of defective parenting: the Children Act 1989 is to be operated in the context of the above policy. Only exceptionally should the State intervene with compulsive powers and then only when a court is satisfied that the significant harm criterion in s 31(2) is made out. Article 8(2) of the European Convention for the Protection of Human Rights and Fundamental Freedoms 1950 and s 31(2) contemplate the exceptional rather than the commonplace.'

11.4 Unidentified abusers

HC **Re CB and JB (Minors) (Care Proceedings: Case Conduct)**
[1998] 2 FCR 313

CB was twice shaken and injured. The court could not tell on the first occasion which parent had done it, but found on the balance of probabilities on the second that it was the mother. Care orders for both children were made.

A finding of fact that one child has been non-accidentally injured by one or both parents while in joint care is sufficient to satisfy the threshold criteria in relation not only to that child but also in relation to a sibling in the parents' joint care at the time who has not suffered injury, notwithstanding that on the evidence the court cannot be satisfied which parent had inflicted the injuries, since the risk of harm to each child from either parent is substantial.

HL *Re O and N* [2003] 1 FLR 1169

In two cases the question arose as to whether a parent who was not positively found to be abusive but who could not be exonerated should be treated as a possible perpetrator at the welfare stage.

The court should consider them a possible perpetrator. It would be grotesque if, because neither parent had been proved to be the perpetrator, the court had to proceed at the welfare stage as though the child were not at risk from either parent, even though one or other of them was the perpetrator of significant harm.

CA *North Yorkshire County Council v SA* [2003] EWCA Civ 839, [2003] 3 FCR 118

An 11-week-old baby suffered serious non-accidental injuries twice. In care proceedings the judge was unable to identify the perpetrator of either injury but did not exclude any of the parents, the maternal grandmother or the night nanny from being the possible perpetrator of the second injury. He asked himself whether he was satisfied that there was no possibility that the possible perpetrator had injured the child.

When attempting to identify the possible perpetrator(s) of non-accidental injuries to a baby or young child when there was no direct evidence of who inflicted the injuries, the correct approach of the court was to apply a test of no real possibility, not a test of no possibility. The test of no possibility was patently too wide and might encompass anyone who had even a fleeting contact with the child in circumstances in which there was the opportunity to cause injuries. The test was whether there was a real possibility or likelihood that one or more of a number of people with access to the child might have caused the injury.

CA *Re K (Non-Accidental Injuries: Perpetrator: New Evidence)*
[2005] 1 FLR 285

The judge in care proceedings could not identify the perpetrator of injuries to the child due to a 'conspiracy of silence' between mother, father and paternal grandmother. He stated that the mother was an 'unwilling conspirator'. The mother was a young Sikh woman who did not speak English. Care orders and freeing orders were made. Later the mother moved to a refuge. She then appealed against the orders, identifying other members of the family in fresh evidence.

It was in the public interest to identify a perpetrator. Despite the freeing order having been made, the matter should not be left open but the children's future reconsidered in the light of this new evidence. It was in the public interest that children have the right, as they grow into adulthood, to know the truth about who injured them while they were children, and why. It was sufficient that the fresh evidence might reasonably lead, on a rehearing, to a finding that the mother could be excluded as a possible perpetrator.

11.5 Balance of probabilities

HL *Re H and others (Minors) (Sexual Abuse: Standard of Proof)* [1996] 1 All ER 1

One child was placed in care on the basis that her step-father had sexually abused her. Later the local authority applied for care orders under s 31(2) CA 1989 for her siblings on the grounds that they were 'likely to suffer significant harm'. The step-father was acquitted of rape. A judge refused to make an order on the basis that he could not be sure to the requisite standard to prove that the first child's allegations were true.

The threshold for s 31(2) was fulfilled if it were shown that there was a real possibility that the child would suffer significant harm. The standard of proof was the ordinary civil standard, i.e. the balance of probabilities. However the more serious or improbable the allegation of abuse, the more convincing was the evidence required to prove the allegation.

A conclusion that a child was likely to suffer harm had to be based on facts, not just suspicion.

HC *Re ET (Serious Injuries: Standard of Proof)* [2003] 2 FLR 1205

Bodey J, considering the standard of proof, restated that the standard of proof is the ordinary civil standard of the balance of probabilities, remembering that the more improbable the event the stronger must be the evidence that it did occur. But the judge added that in this very serious case, the little difference between the civil and criminal standards of proof was 'largely illusory'.

CA *Re B* [2004] Fam Law 565

A child had multiple admissions to hospital for a failure to thrive, and then 11 episodes of potentially life-threatening rigors within six days. On each occasion the mother was present or nearby, but no medical cause was shown. When the child was removed from her presence there were no further rigors. Six experts reported and agreed that infection was the most likely cause of the rigors; two of them opined that mother had deliberately introduced the infection by the cannula into the child, which the mother knew how to use.

Taken alone, the medical evidence was not sufficient to pass the *Re H* balance of probabilities test. However the judge was still entitled to take account of the fact that there was no explanation for the rigors, and to assess the weight and credibility of the non-medical evidence. The totality of the evidence was relevant and cogent and the judge was entitled to rely on it. In family cases the judge was required to ask himself which of two possibilities – human agency or unascertained natural cause – was most likely. If persuaded that it was more likely to be the former, the court was entitled to draw a conclusion adverse to the carer. The evidence was likely to be wider than at a criminal trial and the standard of proof different. Bodey J had applied too high a standard of proof in *Re ET (Serious Injuries: Standard of Proof)* [2003] 2 FLR 1205.

11.6 Notifying the family

HC *Re B (Care Proceedings: Notification of Father without Parental Responsibility)* [1999] 2 FLR 408

An unmarried father applied late in proceedings to be a party to a care case about a child with whom he had little contact.

A father without parental responsibility ought ordinarily to be given the opportunity to be heard before major decisions were taken in relation to his child, and if he wished to participate as a party to care proceedings, he should be permitted to do so unless there was some justifiable reason for not joining him as a party.

HC *Re X (Care: Notice of Proceedings)* [1996] 1 FLR 186

The mother of X was an unmarried Bangladeshi girl aged 17. The father of the child was the mother's brother-in-law. The father did not know that the mother had given birth to a child by him. The local authority sought a care order in respect of X, with a view to an adoptive placement. The mother, supported by the guardian *ad litem*, sought a direction that notice of the proceedings should not be served on the father. The evidence was that if the relationship were to be known, the mother would be ostracised and the overall effect catastrophic.

Rule 4.4(3) of the Family Proceedings Rules 1991 required a father without parental responsibility to be served with notice. Rule 4.8(8), however, conferred upon the court a general discretion to direct that the rule requiring service of notice of the proceedings upon the putative father should be disapplied. In making that decision, the welfare of the child was an important consideration, but not the paramount consideration. The court was entitled to consider, quite independently of the welfare of the child, the effect on the child's family which would be likely if notice of the proceedings were to be served on the putative father. On balance here, no notice should be given.

HC ***Birmingham City Council v S*** [2006] EWHC 3065 (Fam)

A child was fathered by a Muslim couple. The father had not told his parents of the child, and feared ostracism if they found out, although at one point he did say that his mother might put herself forward as a carer. The father was willing to pay maintenance and continue contact. He applied for an order that the local authority, guardian and mother be forbidden to disclose the fact of his fatherhood to them or any other person associated with the proceedings. That application was opposed by the mother, the local authority and the guardian.

The grandparents should be told and the father should have a limited opportunity to do so before the guardian did. On the evidence, it was likely that a person within the father's family would wish to be considered as a potential carer. The child had a right to be brought up within her own family unless there was good reason why not and the paternal family also had a right to put themselves forward as potential carers in order that the child might remain in the family. When practicalities were also considered and the rights of the child, father and paternal grandparents put in the balance, the child's rights prevailed. To deprive a significant member of the wider family of the information that the child, who might otherwise be adopted, existed, was a fundamental step that could only be justified on cogent and compelling grounds – grounds that did not exist here.

11.7 Reopening cases

CA *Re B (Agreed Findings of Fact)* [1998] 2 FLR 968

The mother admitted various facts satisfying the threshold criteria, but denied administering salt to a child. There was a pending prosecution on that allegation. The local authority wanted a 10-day hearing on that issue in the care proceedings before the prosecution. The court allowed it and the mother appealed.

Because of the mother's concessions to the threshold a finding of fact hearing was not needed because it would not alter the protection currently to be given to the children. The case might none the less have to be reopened, as if the mother were later convicted of the criminal charges a new order taking account of that conviction might be needed, and if she were acquitted the authority might wish to have the issue adjudicated by the civil courts.

11.8 Contents of care plans/use of ICOs

Re S (Minors) (Care Order: Implementation of Care Plan) and Re W (Minors: Adequacy of Care Plan) [2002] 1 FCR 815

In the Court of Appeal it had been held that judges should use interim care plans more to ensure that the care plan was suitable and implemented. It was suggested that once a final order was made, key elements of the care plan should be 'starred', and if not implemented the children's guardian should bring the matter back to court. The local authorities appealed. The starred care plan idea had been proposed from fear that the Children Act 1989 was incompatible with Arts 6 and 8 of the European Convention because parents had no way of challenging the implementation of a care plan after final order.

Once a care order was made, the responsibility for the child's care was that of the local authority, not the court.

The CA 1989 was not incompatible with human rights because freestanding applications could be made under the Human Rights Act 1998.

Interim care orders were not to be used as a supervisory role. They could be made if more information was needed before the court could be sure a final order was appropriate. Some uncertainties in the care plan were suitable for sorting out under an interim order with purposive delay. Others frequently had to be worked out after final order.

Lord Nichols

'I consider this judicial innovation passes well beyond the boundary of interpretation. I can see no provision in the Children Act 1989 which lends itself to the interpretation that Parliament was thereby conferring this supervisory function on the court. No such provision was identified by the Court of Appeal. On the contrary, the starring system is inconsistent in an important respect with the scheme of the Children Act 1989. It would constitute amendment of the Children Act 1989, not its interpretation. It would have far-reaching practical ramifications for local authorities and their care of children. The starring system would not come free from additional administrative work and expense. It would be likely to have a material effect on authorities' allocation of scarce financial and other resources. This in turn would affect authorities' discharge of their responsibilities to other children. Moreover, the need to produce a formal report whenever a care plan is significantly departed from, and then await the outcome of any subsequent court proceedings, would affect the whole manner in which authorities discharge, and are able to discharge, their parental responsibilities. These are matters for decision by Parliament, not the courts.'

11.9 Care or supervision?

HC *Re S(J) (A Minor) (Care or Supervision Order)* [1993] 2 FLR
919

The concept of parental responsibility was at the heart of the
difference between a supervision order and a care order. A care
order meant that the local authority could take over virtually
all the parental responsibility functions if it was satisfied that it
was necessary to do so in order to safeguard or promote the
child's welfare. Under s 35 the supervisor had a duty to advise
and assist the supervised child, but no obligation to advise the
parent. The obligation was to operate the supervision order to
make it work, but that was all. There was no obligation to
safeguard or keep the child safe under a supervision order.
That obligation remained with the parent who had parental
responsibility. That was the fundamental difference between
the two orders.

HC *Re B (Care or Supervision Order)* [1996] 2 FLR 693

It could be appropriate to make a full care order even if (i) all
parties agreed that the children should not be removed from
home and (ii) the local authority was seeking a supervision
order, having regard to the fact that the power to remove the
child in an emergency was significantly stronger under the care
order procedure, and that where there was a care order the
local authority had a duty under s 22 of the 1989 Act to
safeguard the child, whereas with a supervision order the duty
to safeguard the child lay with the mother. However, a care
order was a more serious order and should only be made if the
stronger order was necessary for the protection of the child.

11.10 Contact to a child in care

HC *Re P (Minors) (Contact With Children in Care)* [2001] 1 FCR 923

When interpreting the duty to allow parents 'reasonable' contact to a child in care, the duty was to be interpreted objectively. It was not the same as saying contact was at the discretion of a local authority.

QBD *Re M (Care Proceedings: Judicial Review)* [2003] 2 FLR 171

Munby J

'If a baby is to be removed from his mother, one would normally expect arrangements to be made by the local authority to facilitate contact on a regular and generous basis. It is a dreadful thing to take a baby away from a mother; dreadful for the mother, dreadful for the father and dreadful for the baby . . . Those arrangements must be driven by the needs of the family, not stunted by lack of resources. Typically, if this is what the parents want, one will be looking to contact most days of the week and for lengthy periods. And local authorities must be sensitive to the wishes of a mother who wishes to breastfeed and enable her to do so – and when I say breastfeed, I mean just that, I do not mean bottle feeding expressed breast milk. Nothing else will meet the imperative of the European Convention. Contact two or three times a week for a couple of hours at a time is simply not enough if parents reasonably want more.'

Kirklees MBC v S (Contact to New Born Babies) [2006] **2 FLR 333**

Bodey J referred to the above judgment, but qualified it saying that he did not wish to descend from Munby J's observations in *Re M* provided that they are not elevated into principles, and provided it is not understood from them that the words 'most days of the week' imply daily contact including at weekends.

Bodey J

'[N]or do I consider that Munby J's comment that such contact arrangements "must be driven by needs of the family, not stumped by lack of resources", was intended to mean that resources are a wholly irrelevant consideration. It is clear that the practicalities of arranging contact by a mother to a baby have to be borne in mind as part of deciding what one to have contact would constitute reasonable or appropriate contact under section 34 within which decision making process at least some regard must generally be had to the extent to which the quantum of contact would be likely to impose unreasonable burdens either on the foster carer's abilities to sustain it, and/or on the resources of the Local Authority to facilitate it.'

CHAPTER 12

CHALLENGING A LOCAL AUTHORITY'S ACTIONS

Is there a procedural flaw? → YES

↓ NO

Is there an interference with Art 8?

Has it had a detrimental effect on the case?

↓ YES   ↓ NO

NO   YES

Is the interference proportionate and legitimate when weighed against the child's welfare?

YES →

No set aside and no damages

↓ NO

May set aside the order. Damages only if it is just and necessary to offer satisfaction

See cases: *C v Bury Metropolitan Borough Council* (2002); *P v South Gloucestershire County Council* (2007); *Re S (Minors) (Care order: implementation of care plan)* (2002); *Re W (Minors) (Care order: Adequacy of Care Plan)* (2002)

12.1 Alleged breaches of human rights

 C v Bury Metropolitan Borough Council [2002] 2 FLR 868

The local authority sought to remove a child from an unsuitable children's home to a residential school many miles from the mother. The mother was not present at all the meetings concerning the implementation and revision of the care plan, and was not informed of all decisions taken. In particular, she was not told of a decision not to assess her with a view to returning the child to her care. The mother sought a review of the decisions of the local authority under ss 6 and 7 of the Human Rights Act 1998 and Art 8 of the European Convention on the Protection of Human Rights and Fundamental Freedoms 1950 on her own behalf, and on behalf of the child.

Human rights challenges to care plans and placements of children in care should be heard in the Family Division of the High Court. The approach of the court to a challenge to the procedures followed and the care plan adopted should be broader and more investigative than prior to the Human Rights Act 1998.

There were clear procedural flaws in the case management amounting to Article 8 breaches, but they had no detrimental effect on the mother's case, nor were the rights of the child adversely affected, and the decisions of the local authority were, therefore, not set aside for procedural irregularity.

As long as the proposed plans were suitable, the existence of equally suitable alternatives did not entitle the court to interfere with the duty of the local authority to make arrangements for the child's placement. The local authority was acting appropriately and there was no breach of the rights of the child, or his mother, in the plans put forward.

P v South Gloucestershire County Council [2007] EWCA Civ 2

The care plan gave the mother six months to prove her parenting capacity otherwise the child would be placed for adoption. Within that period she made threats of serious harm to others and possibly towards herself and the baby. The baby was lawfully removed. The local authority, however, were found to have breached her human rights because she was not present at a meeting where the decision to change the care plan was made. A declaration without damages was made. The mother appealed, seeking damages.

The European Court of Human Rights generally favoured an award of damages in cases where local authorities had infringed the rights of parents under Art 8 by shortcomings in the procedures they used to take children into care. Satisfaction to the person whose rights had been infringed must be 'just', and only if it were 'necessary' in order to afford satisfaction should an award of damages be made.

The breach here however was not significant and the distress the mother had felt was due to the lawful removal, not breach of her procedural rights. The local authority had decided not to involve her because of her aggression. The mother was not entitled to compensation.

Haringey London Borough Council v C (E, E, F and High Commissioner of Republic of Kenya Intervening) [2005] 2 FLR 47

A couple with firm fundamental Christian beliefs 'acquired' a child after a period of infertility, claiming it to be a miracle baby. DNA tests showed that the child was not theirs and that the true parents were in Kenya and could not be found. The couple wished to keep the child and cited their right to religious freedom and their right to respect for their family and private life. An adoptive placement was available.

Despite the respect given to private and family life, to freedom of thought, conscience and religion and any individual belief system, the law did not give religious belief or birthright a pre-eminent place in the balance of factors that comprised welfare. If the views of the couple were to be sanctioned, it would be virtually impossible for them to modify their position beyond their beliefs and the child would have to be encapsulated within that belief system and his future founded upon a lie. A placement with them would thus be contrary to the child's interests.

12.2 Procedure for raising human rights breaches

HL *Re S (Minors) (Care Order: Implementation of Care Plan); Re W (Minors) (Care Order: Adequacy of Care Plan)* [2002] UKHL 10, [2002] 1 FLR 815

In the first case the care plan included a substantial package of support and rehabilitation for the mother which was not implemented. She had no remedy to force that provision under the CA 1989 and it was alleged that as she had no remedy, there was a breach of Art 6 which includes the right to bring issues about civil rights to a fair hearing.

Whilst it is true that the CA 1989 did not produce a remedy, there was no Art 6 breach because an alternative mechanism was available under s 7 Human Rights Act 1998. The fact that a given statute does not provide a remedy does not make that statue incompatible *per se* with the European Convention. The absence in the Children Act 1989 of effective machinery for protecting the civil rights of young children with no parent or guardian was a statutory lacuna, not a statutory incompatibility.

HC | ***Re L (Care Proceedings: Human Rights Claims)*** **[2003] 2 FLR 160**

In a care case in the Family Proceedings Court, the local authority originally planned for a family placement, then changed the plan to adoption. The mother claimed a human rights breach and that claim was transferred to the High Court whilst the substantive case remained in the FPC.

If care proceedings were at an end, the remedy for a human rights breach was a free-standing application under s 7 Human Rights Act 1998. If care proceedings were ongoing, the court hearing the case had jurisdiction to hear the human rights aspect.

12.3 Negligence claims against a local authority

HL *X v Bedfordshire CC and others* [1995] 2 FLR 276

In a number of joined appeals the plaintiffs alleged that they had suffered damage because the public authorities had been negligent. Some cases involved abuse of children, others alleged failure to supply proper education.

In the abuse cases: there is no common-law duty of care on the authority in relation to the performance of its statutory duty to protect children. Such a duty would cut across the whole system set up for the protection of children at risk, since the task involved was extraordinarily delicate and the imposition of damages might cause the authorities to adopt a more cautious and defensive approach. There was similarly no common-law duty of care in the exercise of its duties relating to children with special educational needs within the Education Act 1981.

HL *Barrett v Enfield LBC* [1999] 2 FLR 426

The plaintiff sought damages, alleging that whilst in care he had not been given the care a parent would give and had been left with alcohol problems, a tendency to self-harm, behavioural problems and a failed marriage. The claim was struck out as having no cause of action and that decision was appealed against.

Once a child was actually taken into care the local authority owed him a duty of care. The case should be heard on its merits.

HL *W and others v Essex County Council and another* [2000] I FLR 657

A family sought damages for psychiatric injury. The parents as foster carers to the local authority said they would not foster children who were known or suspected of being sexual abusers. Such a child was placed with them and was said to have abused the children of the family. The parents had been told they could not sue for psychiatric injury flowing from their discovery of this, and appealed.

It was arguable that there was breach of a duty of care. It would be difficult but not impossible to say that the parents were 'primary' victims of psychiatric injury as required by law for damages. They should not be barred from pursuing it at trial.

HC *A and B v Essex County Council* [2003] I FLR 615

Prospective adopters were approved for a child with mild emotional disturbance. The local authority placed with them a child with serious behavioural difficulties, including severe violence towards the sister also placed with him. The parents claimed damages in respect of the authority's negligence in failing to provide relevant information about the child. The mother's claim included damages for psychiatric illness alleged to have been caused by the impact of the behaviour.

The local authority owed a justiciable common law duty of care to the parents, which included taking all reasonable steps to provide all relevant information about the children. They had breached their duty by not doing so. Psychiatric injury was foreseeable in all the circumstances of the particular case. The damages only ran from placement to adoption since by adoption the couple had all the relevant information and chose to proceed anyway.

CHAPTER 13

ADOPTION AND SPECIAL GUARDIANSHIP

Adoption gives total security and makes the child part of the new family, and places adopters in parental control of the child: *Re H (Adoption: parental agreement)* (1982)

In general judges would be expected to inform fathers of adoption proceedings unless for good reason it was inappropriate. This may depend on whether there was Art 8 family life between father and child: *Re H: Re G (Adoption: Consultation of unmarried fathers)* (2001)

Adoption: Key Points

Under the AA 1976, in withholding consent a parent may be acting unreasonably even if there is no element of culpability or reprehensible conduct in his decision. The test whether the refusal is unreasonable is an objective one to be made in all the circumstances of the case.
Re W (an infant) (1971)

The types of cases in which SGOs may be appropriate
(i) Older children who do not wish to be legally separated from their birth families.
(ii) Children being cared for on a permanent basis by members of their wider birth family.
(iii) Children in some minority ethnic communities who have religious and cultural difficulties with adoption as it is set out in law.
(iv) Unaccompanied asylum-seeking children who need secure, permanent homes, but have strong attachments to their families abroad.

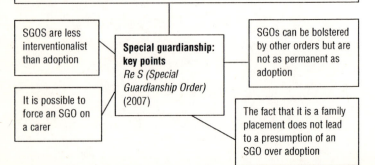

SGOS are less interventionalist than adoption

Special guardianship: key points
Re S (Special Guardianship Order) (2007)

SGOs can be bolstered by other orders but are not as permanent as adoption

It is possible to force an SGO on a carer

The fact that it is a family placement does not lead to a presumption of an SGO over adoption

13.1 Benefits of adoption

CA *Re H (Adoption: Parental Agreement)* (1982) 3 FLR 476

A mother with alcohol addition was unable to care for her child but also unable to give him up for adoption. Her consent was dispensed with.

Ormrod J

'What do the adoptive parents gain by an adoption order over and above what they have already got on a long-term fostering basis? To that the answer is always the same – and it is always a good one – adoption gives us total security and makes the child part of our family, and places us in parental control of the child; long-term fostering leaves us exposed to changes of view of the local authority, it leaves us exposed to applications, and so on, by the natural parent. That is a perfectly sensible and reasonable approach; it is far from being only an emotive one.'

13.2 The rights of unmarried parents

HC *Re H: Re G (Adoption: Consultation of Unmarried Fathers)* [2001] 1 FLR 646

In both cases mothers placed babies for adoption on the basis that the fathers would not be told. In the first case the couple had cohabited and already had an older child, with whom the father had contact. The pregnancy had been concealed. In the second case there had been no cohabitation and the couple had lost touch. The question was whether the fathers had to be informed about adoption proceedings.

In general, judges would be expected to inform fathers of adoption proceedings unless for good reason it was inappropriate. In the first case there was family life which gave rise to Art 8 rights and the father should be told. In the second case Art 8 was not an issue and he need not be told.

HC *Z County Council v R* [2001] 1 FLR 365

After a concealed pregnancy the mother placed the child for adoption. She was adamant that her family must not know. At the freeing order stage the question arose as to whether any of her family should be asked if they could offer the child a home.

Without looking at the European Convention, the adoption rules in force at the time empowered consultation with the family but in this case did not require it, since there was no reason to doubt the truth of the mother's statement that the family could not care.

Article 8 however was engaged as there was family life between father and child. However it was proportionate to interfere with that to preserve confidentiality in order to protect the mother's Art 8 right to a private life.

Re J (Adoption: Contacting Father) [2003] 1 **FLR 933**

The mother gave birth at 16. She had been seeing the father for two years and their relationship ended just after she became pregnant. They had had no contact with each other since then and the father knew nothing of the pregnancy or birth. After placement for adoption and assurances of confidentiality, the child was diagnosed with cystic fibrosis, a genetic disease. The local authority wanted to notify the father.

The relationship did not have sufficient constancy to create *de facto* family ties for the purposes of establishing 'family life' between the father and child. The exceptional facts meant the general rule that fathers should be informed of applications to adopt or free for adoption did not apply. The potentially damaging consequences to the mother of the news leaking out into the community should the father or his family be informed of the birth outweighed any potential advantage to the child of informing the father. A failure to inform the father that he might be a carrier of cystic fibrosis was not an interference with his right to respect for private life under Art 8 of the European Convention.

13.3 The old test for dispensing with consent

HL *Re W (An Infant)* [1971] 2 All ER 49

A mother gave up a child for adoption. Much later regretting this, she sought to withhold her consent to the adoption. The mother was said to be genuine in her desire to care, but the move would not be in the best interest of the child.

In withholding consent a parent may be acting unreasonably even if there is no element of culpability or reprehensible conduct in this decision. The test whether the refusal is unreasonable is an objective one to be made in all the circumstances of the case.

13.4 Special guardianship

CA *Re S (Special Guardianship Order)* [2007] EWCA Civ 54

The mother agreed that the child should stay with the foster carer, with whom the mother had a very close relationship. The foster carer sought an adoption order, the court made an SGO.

→

Re AJ (Adoption Order or Special Guardianship Order) [2007] EWCA Civ 55, see below.

CA *Re M-J (A Child)* [2007] EWCA Civ 56

The Court of Appeal dealt with three SGO cases. The judgments of the other two refer back to the material below.

- The types of cases in which SGOs may be appropriate
  (i) Older children who do not wish to be legally separated from their birth families.
  (ii) Children being cared for on a permanent basis by members of their wider birth family.
  (iii) Children in some minority ethnic communities, who have religious and cultural difficulties with adoption as it is set out in law.
  (iv) Unaccompanied asylum-seeking children who need secure, permanent homes, but have strong attachments to their families abroad.

- The key question which the court will be obliged to ask itself in every case in which the question of adoption as opposed to special guardianship arises will be: which order will better serve the welfare of this particular child?
- The court must seek the least interventionalist order to comply with Art 8. In some cases this will tip the balance in favour of an SGO over adoption.
- The weight to be given to the effect of adoption on family relationships depends on the facts of each case.
- After an SGO a parent does not require leave to apply for any s 8 order other than residence. SGOs can be 'bolstered' by the use of a s 91(14) order, but special guardianship does not always provide the same permanency of protection as adoption.
- It is possible to make an SGO against the wishes of the future carers.

CA Re AJ (Adoption Order or Special Guardianship Order) [2007] EWCA Civ 55

A child had been placed with its aunt and uncle for over six years. They sought adoption and preferred a care order to an SGO so that the local authority was under a duty to assist with repeated applications. An adoption order was made.

Special guardianship orders had not effectively replaced adoption orders in cases where children were to be placed permanently within their wider families. It cannot be said – in cases under the 1976 Act – that a parent is not unreasonable in withholding consent just because there is now an SGO as an alternative to adoption.

CA Re M-J (A Child) [2007] EWCA Civ 56

A recovered drug addict mother agreed that the child should remain with carers under an SGO. An adoption order was made.

It was not helpful to approach a case on the basis that that an SGO was the preferred option over adoption unless there were cogent reasons against adoption. It would be wrong for a court to feel constrained to make a special guardianship order rather than an adoption order on the basis that the former was less interventionist: such would be a clear derogation from the paramountcy of the welfare principle.

INDEX